NIGHT FEVER
interior design for
bars and clubs

Frame Publishers
Amsterdam

Birkhäuser – Publishers for Architecture
Basel • Boston • Berlin

Contents

4   Picturing Ecstasy

12   Night Fever

14   Academy, Canberra, Australia

22   Drop Kick, Tokyo, Japan

30   J-Pop Café, Taipei, Taiwan

38   Bed Supperclub, Bangkok, Thailand

46   Touch, Hyderabad, India

54   Coconclub, Moscow, Russia

62   buzADA, Istanbul, Turkey

70   Gravity, Vilnius, Lithuania

78   Club Tallinn, Tartu, Estonia

86   ABSOLUT ICEBAR, Jukkasjârvi, Sweden

94   Club Passage, Vienna, Austria

102   Club Stromovka, Prague, Czech Republic

110   Divina, Milan, Italy

118   CocoonClub, Frankfurt am Main, Germany

126   BarRouge, Basel, Switzerland

134   Lucky Strike Bars, Geneva and Lausanne, Switzerlan

142   Jimmy Woo, Amsterdam, the Netherlands

150   Sinners, Amsterdam, the Netherlands

158   Supperclubs, Amsterdam, the Netherlands and

20 22 24 26 28 30 32 34 36

60 62 64 66 68 70 72 74 76

100 102 104 106 108 110 112 114 116

140 142 144 146 148 150 152 154 156

180 182 184 186 188 190 192 194 196

220 222 224 226 228 230 232 234 236

260 262 264 266 268 270 272 274 276

300 302 304 306 308 310 312

Supperclub, Rome, Italy
166 Now & Wow, Rotterdam, the Netherlands
174 Culture Club, Ghent, Belgium
182 Kant, Brugge, Belgium
190 Oven, Barcelona, Spain
198 Cab, Paris, France
206 Cinnamon Club Bar, London, England

214 Kabaret's Prophecy, London, England
222 Le Carrousel, Nantes, France
226 Rehab, Leeds, England
234 Babushka, Manchester, England
242 Collage Bar, Glasgow, Scotland
246 D-Edge, São Paulo, Brazil
254 Crobar NY, New York City, USA

262 Guvernment, Toronto, Canada
270 Loft, Caracas, Venezuela
278 The Spider Club, New York, USA
282 Sound-Bar, Chicago, USA
290 Thin, San Diego, USA
298 Project Credits and Addresses
312 Colophon

Picturing ecstasy

'Going out' means more than simply leaving your house; it's about jumping into another world – a place filled with fantasy and magic.

When people say they're 'going out', where and what do they leave, and where do they go? For starters, they go out of the house, out of a dull evening spent in front of the television, out of their everyday lives, out of their problems, and out of their established mindsets. They enter another realm, a place we call 'nightlife': the polar opposite of ordinary 'daylife'.

Russian thinker Mikhail Bakhtin traced this dichotomy back to the Middle Ages, a time in which citizens lived two lives: 'the *official* life, monolithically serious and gloomy, subjugated to a strict hierarchical order, full of terror, dogmatism, reverence and piety' and 'the *life of the carnival square*, free and unrestricted, full of ambivalent laughter, blasphemy, the profanation of everything sacred, full of debasing and obscenities, familiar contact with everyone and everything'.

Like nightlife today, Bakhtin's carnival was unabashedly corporeal, a celebration of the gluttonous pleasures of the body: drink, dance and sex – the three-letter word that fuels so many of evening's pastimes. The carnivals of yore happened once a year; today we go to bed each night knowing that somewhere, *out there*, a party's going on. That free and unrestricted world – where you can go to reinvent yourself and behave in ways that would shock your boss and shame your family – exists without interruption.

It feeds on an underground energy that surfaces every night in millions of nightspots around the world, ready to be tapped into at any time. People may think that they are going out in search of other people, but they're also in search of themselves. For the places we hang out in and, by extension, the scenes we take part in give us a strong sense of our own footprints in the world, certainly as much as we get from going to work or spending time at home.

Cocoons, islands, underground bunkers, skyscrapers: the night world has expanded far beyond the borders of the standard corner pub or the pedestrian discotheque. Going out is about fantasy and magic, and the right location – under the Venezuelan stars, in a massive grain warehouse – casts a spell on us immediately. We know that here the rules that govern our daytime lives are suspended, if only for a few precious hours until the sun comes up again.

People don't 'do' much in bars and nightclubs. They buy drinks, talk and dance. Sometimes they sit. Sometimes they stand. A purely literal analysis of the functions of such venues is, therefore, a trap.
What clubbers and bar-hoppers are really there to do is to watch and listen, to take in the music, the crowd, the lighting and all the other stimuli; to be transformed and entertained.

Socializing is, by nature, a collective experience; interior designs that address the needs of groups (and not just individuals) are bound to be more successful. Traffic flow, accessibility of bars and toilets, and composition of seating areas are critical factors for programming these spaces.

People go out to be with groups of other people: friends, strangers, a mix.

When asked what makes a favourite nightspot so special, clubbers invariably put 'the crowd' near the top of the list.

People-watching, people-meeting: successful bars and clubs take these strongly into account and create strategies to facilitate human interaction where possible. Proportion is key. If a space is too big, groups of strangers are likely to remain disparate entities. Too small, and everyone is lost in one great sea of bodies.

Composed of equal parts fashion and theatre, the best spaces teeter on the edge of the surreal, where the order of daylife is abandoned, obsolete.

About the author

Matthew Stewart is a freelance writer and designer living and working in San Francisco. His work has appeared in several magazines, including *Frame, Interior Design, ReadyMade, Vitals, Surface, Butt,* and *Baby,* for which he served as editor and designer. Prior to that, he worked for a digital design consultancy in San Francisco and London developing brands, strategies, and content. He has a degree in English Literature from Harvard University, and studied three-dimensional design at the Gerrit Rietveld Academie in Amsterdam.

Night Fever

Jet-setting DJs and expanding club franchises have transformed going out from
a local to a global enterprise. Interiors have followed suit, with entrepreneurs
bringing not only the top DJs but also the latest trends to their projects.
And they have an audience in the increasingly well-informed clubbing
bourgeoisie who have had a taste of the best the world has to offer and want
it available in their own back yards.

Hot right now: big prints on wallpapers and screens, domestic furniture
and accents, intelligent lighting systems, strong graphic logos and identities,
membership-only spaces and biomorphic structures.

Nightlife entrepreneurs know that interiors date quickly and wear out even
faster. Successful spaces have to be resilient, with durable materials and
easily updated styles and details.

Disco balls are back with a vengeance, but today they're often symbolic
(oversized, oddly positioned, used as signs) as much as functional.
Designers toy with them as a shorthand way of signalling this space
is part of the night universe.

People may not notice the details of interiors, especially in bigger spaces, but
they can feel them. Crowds of people tend to obscure any interior elements
that fall below eye level. The solution: details in the air, on the ceiling and in
the higher reaches of a space.

Bigger isn't always better: a growing trend towards smaller clubs with more
select crowds is proving that there's room in the nightlife ecosystem for more
modest ventures.

People have been going out for centuries. People will always go out.
Why then is there such tremendous turnover in bars and nightclubs, with
new ones sprouting everyday as formerly successful venues close their doors?
The answer, in a word, is fashion.

When a place becomes aligned with a scene, a look, a moment, it's a blessing
and a curse: a blessing because it ensures instant crowds and a strong sense
of identity, a curse because this very alignment can prove to be an anchor too
heavy to weather the shifting tides of taste.

Matthew Stewart

Using luxurious finishes and modern furnishings, SJB Interiors cranks up the glam heat at Canberra's **Academy.**

In the '70s, begins Andrew Parr, offering a chronological tour of nightclub design, 'glamour reigned in shimmering and glitzy materials'. In the '80s, he says, it was 'large mega-clubs with raw and burnished metals against cool colours' that set the pace, while the clubs of the '90s were 'more eclectic in design, using found objects, setting rococo against modern'. And now? Parr points to 'warm colour selections, opulent materials and design looking to futurism for inspiration', and mentions Far Eastern influences as well. Parr, principal of SJB Interiors, believes these trends originate from changes in music styles and the moods they have created. Thus, as music and clubs

resurface – after a decade spent underground emulating warehouse-fuelled rave-style parties – places like SJB's Academy in Canberra are taking design cues from day spas and boutiques, using luxurious finishes and sleekly contemporary furnishings to crank up the glam heat.

The Academy took root when SJB's clients purchased the landmark Cinema Centre, Canberra's first movie theatre, to house their new club. Erected in 1966, 'the venue pays homage to all that was hip and happening in the '60s', says the designer. Parr and his team merged the cinema's original elements – such as a broad staircase featuring original timber strapping and playfully

Previous page and top: Ross Lovegrove's BD Love Lamps are a distinctive feature of the main room. Doubling as couches, they hurl beacons of light into the air. The mirror ball above responds with hundreds of pin spots that cascade over the sleek surfaces of the interior. Above: The Pod is a private VIP lounge that can be rented out for special events. Arriving guests spot the logo on glass entrance doors.

angular walls in the mezzanine and theatre – with decidedly modern finishes and larger-than-life lighting and furnishings. Just enough retro styling shines through to add the tiniest element of camp, à la Austin Powers, to the flavour, making the space well suited to the Aussie clubber's temperament.
SJB applied the same formula, with different results, to the various areas of the cinema to create three distinctive club experiences. Says Parr: 'A series of spaces were outlined in the brief: a smaller, intimate cocktail lounge which has views over the dance floor; a large dance floor volume; and smaller, cocoon-like rooms.' These were executed, respectively, as the Candy Bar, the main

room, and The Pod. 'The Candy Bar is an ultra-sleek and sophisticated cocktail lounge, which hovers above the main room,' says Parr. 'You can kick back and relax while enjoying expansive views of the main room via the glass wall.' The name of the bar hints at its former life as the cinema's refreshment stand. Guests still flock here for drinks, but gone is the counter of old. In its place, a mosaic bar rises from a mosaic floor. Above, visually noting both the '60s genre of the space and its disco heritage, are two mirror-ball pendant lights, by Tom Dixon for DeDeCe. In a motif that is repeated throughout the club, the bar features uplighters. SJB opted for this type of illumination, says Parr,

Clockwise from top left: Tom Dixon's mirror-ball pendants, designed for DeDeCe, accentuate the '60s glamour and disco heritage of the main room. Bars lit from below are intended, according to Parr, 'to suggest a weightlessness, or levity'. It's the kind of lighting, he says, that 'creates the perfect opportunity to show off those new Manolos'. The toilets are essential to the club experience. 'These spaces are flowing spaces; curved tiled edges reflect the seamless, smooth theme.'

'to suggest a weightlessness, or levity, and to create the perfect opportunity to show off those new Manolos'. Introduced in the bar are the strong furnishings of the club; particularly striking are the bolt-like Expresso stools, from Space, and Korban Flaubert's mesh drum tables, another DeDeCe product. In the main room, Ross Lovegrove's BD Love Lamps, which double as couches, aim needle-like beacons of light at the ceiling above the dance floor. The ceiling aims a volley of lights right back, sending beams sliding across the silky surfaces. 'The room becomes endless, as light skips and twirls over the seamless mosaic bars and the gold-flecked resin floors,' says Parr. 'Every surface is smooth and continuous, providing a sumptuous array of booths, banquettes and bars over which the Academy's A-List can drape themselves.' Those on the A-Plus List are welcome in The Pod, a VIP lounge that is rented out for private events. It's hard to beat Parr's loving description of The Pod: 'Liquid leather banquettes wrap around the walls in a fluid gesture of comfort and luxury, and loose furniture looks like a giant-scale exhibition of contemporary jewellery.' Seamless finishes and references to luxury, along with the abstract furniture forms that dot the floors, seem drawn from the world of Gucci belts and Fendi bags, rather than being simply the next step in the

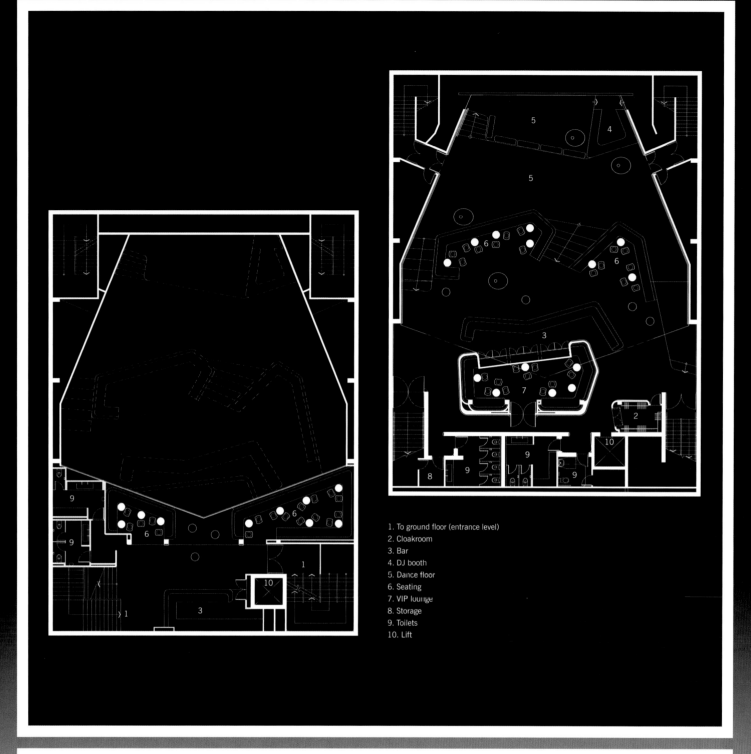

1. To ground floor (entrance level)
2. Cloakroom
3. Bar
4. DJ booth
5. Dance floor
6. Seating
7. VIP lounge
8. Storage
9. Toilets
10. Lift

Left: Basement level 1. Right: Basement level 2.

evolution of nightclub interiors. This synthesis is in keeping with Parr's multi-sensory concept of the ideal nightclub: 'The perfect club transports you to new experiences; it should have a series of spaces that allow a journey through colour, light and music, with combinations of neutral zones and high-feature-design areas to exhilarate and stimulate the senses.' Given these criteria, Parr has come very close to achieving perfection in his own terms.

Left: SJB's designers note favourite components of the Academy interior, all of which appear in the main-room bar and throughout the space: smooth, seamless corners; a sense of theatre; and surface contrasts that pit hard against soft and reflective against non-reflective. Right: The club's strong graphic-identity system brands the interior as well as flyers and other promotional materials.

'The perfect club transports you to new experiences; it should have a series of spaces that allow a journey through colour, light and music.' Andrew Parr

In describing The Pod, Parr is effusive about 'liquid leather banquettes that wrap around the walls in a fluid gesture of comfort and luxury' and 'loose furniture that looks like a giant-scale exhibition of contemporary jewellery'. The look is leavened by 'bangle-like' screens and 'curious shag-pile installations' with integrated fibre-optic lighting.

To seduce Tokyo patrons into enjoying a night at **Drop Kick**, Glamorous gave the tiny bar a generous jolt of sexy energy.

Though the name of Drop Kick, the dark and diminutive year-old bar in Tokyo's bustling Roppongi district, is taken from a professional wrestling move, it's unlikely that patrons entering the space will be visited by images of corpulent men in multicoloured tights. Instead, Yasumichi Morita and Akihiro Fujii – the design team at Glamorous, the Japanese outfit that created the bar – put together a look that is entirely *femme fatale*, with an interior intended, in Morita's own words, to 'knock out the people who visit it'.

Given the high concentration of flashy bars and nightspots in the district, Glamorous took extra steps to attract the attention of passers-by. 'I thought the bar should have a very catchy façade, because there are a thousand clubs or bars with garish signs in the neighbourhood,' says Morita. 'I did something no one else in the world has ever done: I hung a giant mirror ball outside the bar.' His glittering, impossible-to-miss globe is an eye-grabber that, according to the designer, symbolizes the bar. The blanket of lights from the enormous mirror ball – 900 millimetres in diameter – in the front window shines out into the street, introducing the movement and energy of the club before visitors have even set foot inside.

To seduce patrons into enjoying a night at Drop Kick, Morita and his team

Previous page: Designer Yasumichi Morita of Glamorous believes that perfection marred by imperfection can reinforce the charm of a space. 'I left the ceiling of Drop Kick exposed and just painted it,' he says, adding that a unique flaw 'increases the appeal of each of the bars'. Above: In dreaming up elements for an alluring interior, Morita was captivated by a mental image of women's legs, which he translated, rather literally, into acrylic columns with fishnet stockings stretched over their opaque cores.

gave the tiny space a generous jolt of sexy energy. The designer explains that, while drumming up concepts for a blatantly alluring interior, 'women's legs in fishnet tights flashed into my mind'. He interpreted his idea as stockinged legs that form processions of light columns along the walls, defining the entrance area and two nooks, and backing the bar. Each column incorporates an actual fishnet stocking sandwiched between a frosted acrylic pipe and a clear acrylic pipe. The lights within slowly change colours – red, blue and purple – providing almost imperceptible chromatic shifts in mood as the night goes on. Morita says that 'the rest followed naturally' from the leggy columns. Glittery

crimson floor tiles evoke images of rouged cheeks and glossy lips, while crocodile-embossed black leather on bench seating, bar front and cylindrical bar stools suggests handbags, or perhaps thigh boots, depending on the type of woman one has in mind.

In contrast with the girlishness of other details, the bulky polished-granite bar top reflects a rugged squareness. The only concession to the dominant theme is the crosshatched pattern carved into the surface, another reference to stretchy fishnet tights. The same pattern also makes appearances in the bathroom and on the steel cage in the front window.

Top and bottom left: Frosted-glass tabletops with mirrored hemispheres mounted underneath rest on stainless-steel legs. Lights integrated into the floor bounce off each mirror ball, creating a sea of movement around the bar.
Right: In the front window, a mirror ball 90 cm in diameter acts as dynamic signage for Drop Kick, reflecting, even from a distance, the animated atmosphere and energy of the bar.

'I did something no one else in the world has ever done: I hung a giant mirror ball outside the bar.'

Yasumichi Morita

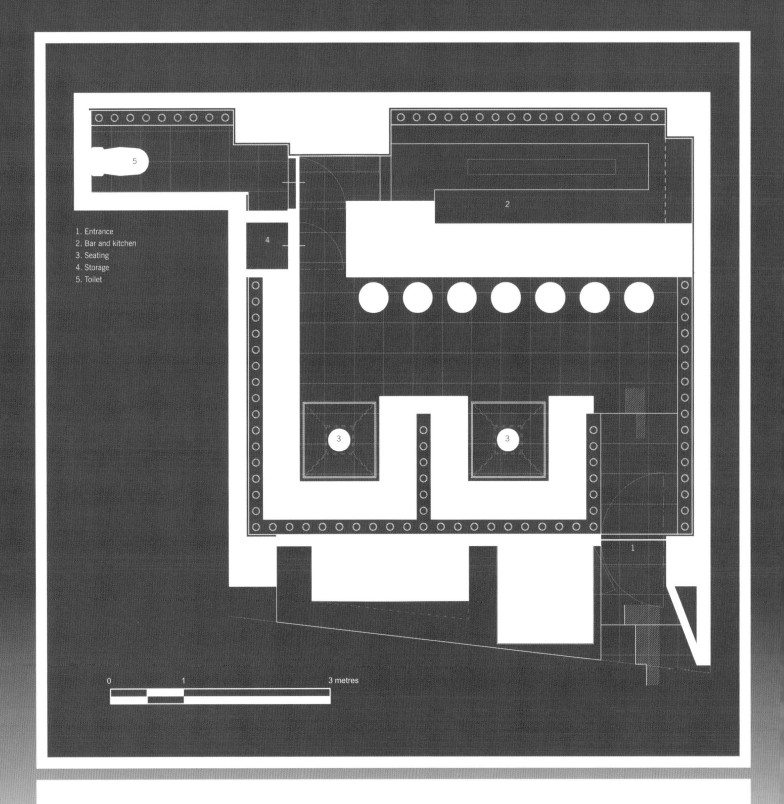

1. Entrance
2. Bar and kitchen
3. Seating
4. Storage
5. Toilet

0   1   3 metres

The square simplicity of the bar resurfaces in the design of frosted-glass tabletops mounted on stainless-steel legs in the two niches. Smaller mirrored hemispheres mounted beneath the tabletops beam forth scattered pinpricks of light cast by specially integrated lamps set into the floor under each table. A soundtrack of '70s and '80s pop (think Marvin Gaye, Bay City Rollers and Van Morrison) spills forth from the speakers. Though not cutting-edge, the music is appropriate: yet another example of the oft-encountered – and slightly estranging – Japanese re-contextualization of mainstream Americana. Squeezing everything into Drop Kick's scant 35 square meters was not easy,

and ending up with a unique identity and a strong result required a design team with a visionary, hand-tailored approach. Morita offers a frank assessment of his work. 'I believe my design should be *haute couture* for each project,' he says. 'But I am an interior designer, not an artist.' As a businessman, he accepts a certain amount of responsibility for the financial success of his clients. Since Drop Kick is nearly doubling the profit made by surrounding bars, according to Morita, his team has obviously taken that responsibility seriously. 'The clients had already decided the location when they asked me to create a cool and groovy bar,' he continues. 'People are

Above and following page left: According to Morita, both surfaces and furniture flowed from the decision to evoke a glamorous woman. Glittering deep-red floor tiles suggest rouge and lipstick, while crocodile-embossed black leather on bench seating, bar front and cylindrical bar stools brings handbags – or perhaps thigh-high boots – to mind.

always looking for new, interesting places to add to their list of Tokyo favourites.' Tiny but memorable, Drop Kick seems to have assured its position on many such lists for the foreseeable future.

Right: Drop Kick mixes its dark and sexy atmosphere with American pop music from the '80s, producing a winning combination for the club's Japanese audience.

Japanese food, kimono patterns and pop divas: Fantastic Design Works brings **J-Pop Café** – the last word in Japanese clubbing – to Taipei.

Katsunori Suzuki, visionary designer at Fantastic Design Works, says that the interiors he created for two J-Pop Cafés in Tokyo display a 'bio-future' style. 'Nowadays, buildings are constructed from concrete, iron, steel and wood,' he says. 'I imagined a future in which biotechnology would enable material from trees or plants – in its natural form – to be used as a building material.' Interestingly, the results weren't so much organic in their usage of materials as they were organic-looking: soft, curvaceous, glowing interiors fused technology into seamless walls. But for the most recent addition to the J-Pop empire, this one in Taipei, the designer departs from the space-age formula to provide

a sophisticated venue with retooled traditional Japanese motifs, a reminder to visitors that J-Pop is, after all, a cultural product.

Spread over two floors in the chic entertainment complex Bistro 98, J-Pop opens with a dazzling entrance area. Dozens of mirror balls, half submerged in the ceiling, send thousands of spots scampering around the room. The lighting, which greets visitors as they step out of the lift, is intensely pink. Several counters display music and related Japanese paraphernalia for sale. A uniformed attendant welcomes guests and, with a wave of the hand, opens sliding doors that lead to a glittering passageway, whose walls and ceiling are

Previous page: A colourful printed screen featuring a motif of the type found on traditional silk kimonos – but stylized in a contemporary pop-graphic manner – adorns the wall behind the steel-plate and concrete spiral staircase that links J-Pop's two floors. Above: Visitors to J-Pop are immersed in a world pulsing with Japanese pop music. The moving image is ubiquitous, most notably in projections that fill the mirror-lined void between the sixth and seventh floors.

clad in mirrored signatures of stars who have visited J-Pop.
The entrance tunnel opens onto a row of individual booths veiled by semi-transparent, steel-mesh curtains. Each booth features an interactive monitor that plays DVDs of Japanese pop-music videos. This is the entertainment at the heart of the J-Pop café, a concept Suzuki quite succinctly summarizes as 'a café serving creative Japanese food where customers keep up to speed with the world of Japanese pop music'. The atmosphere seems to stem not from the nightclubs of today, but from early-20th-century Japanese teahouses, where guests were secluded in private chambers to be entertained by geishas

playing musical instruments and making conversation. The only difference is that J-Pop's geishas are two-dimensional screen images of Japanese divas. The moving image is ubiquitous, from the screens in the booths to – most notably – the projections that fill the void between the sixth and seventh floors. Images reflected in the mirror-lined void seem to go on and on in a dizzying illusion of endless repetition. The net effect is a shared group experience that emerges from what is essentially several smaller groups having private experiences.
In the Tokyo locations, the emphasis of the J-Pop café lies on the 'Pop'

Food is served in the main hall at slick black tables surrounded by white Panton chairs. Here unfussy black and white furniture cedes centre stage to video imagery and lighting.

The only difference is that J-Pop's geishas are two-dimensional screen images of Japanese divas.

Intense pink light and disco balls partially embedded in the ceiling set the tone in the dramatic entrance area, where several counters display Japanese pop music and paraphernalia for sale. Opposite page, left: A mirrored hallway connecting the entrance area to the first floor creates a brief sensation of disorientation between the two zones. Etched into the mirrors are signatures of stars who have visited J-Pop.

'I imagined a future in which biotechnology would enable material from trees or plants – in its natural form – to be used as a building material.' Katsunori Suzuki

Right: The close correlation between music and design visible at the J-Pop Café is what Suzuki sees as a natural synergy. 'One might posit that music, fashion, interior and graphic design have a correlated relationship in that they emerge, grow, evolve and expand at roughly the same pace.'

component of the name, but in Taiwan, the 'J', or Japanese, element, which is largely responsible for the café's draw, is accentuated by a décor that is doubly exotic to Western eyes. On the ceiling, a delicate but rather simple line drawing takes its inspiration from floral patterns found in traditional Japanese tattoos. And lining the back wall, behind the steel-plate and concrete spiral staircase linking the two floors, is a dramatic printed screen featuring a colourful motif of the type found on traditional silk kimonos. The even tones and simplified lines of the digital illustration demonstrate J-Pop café's unique positioning of Japanese culture: shogun images for the *Lost in Translation* set.

Food is served downstairs in the main hall, at gleaming black tables surrounded by Panton chairs. Here, as elsewhere, Suzuki keeps the furniture simple, light and modern, while restricting the palette to black and white. This puts the focus on the ceiling and wall prints, the video images and the vivid pink lighting, which refers back to the entrance and creates, says Suzuki, 'a fantasy-like and slightly punkish image'.

Such a close relationship between design and music comes naturally to Suzuki, who sees strong ties between the two disciplines. 'One might posit that music, fashion, interior and graphic design have a corollary relationship,

Vivid lighting adds splashes of colour to areas not dominated by video images. Suzuki speaks of 'a fantasy-like and slightly punkish image'.

in that they emerge, grow, evolve and expand at roughly the same pace,' says Suzuki, 'which is why I assert that even if one wanted to separate them, they cannot be completely separated.' Thankfully, visitors to J-Pop – where music and design are harmoniously interwoven – are not faced with that dilemma.

Right: The entrance tunnel feeds visitors into an area of booth seating set off by semi-transparent steel-mesh curtains. Each booth features an interactive monitor that plays DVDs of pop-music videos; this is the heart of the J-Pop Café experience.

Sitting in Bangkok's **Bed Supperclub**, you could be anywhere in the world. It's the service that makes this restaurant-cum-club, created by Orbit Design Studio, unmistakably Thai.

Though the dining concept behind Bed Supperclub in Bangkok was inspired by owner Paris Bantra's visits to the Supperclub in Amsterdam, the Southeast Asian interpretation actually traces its roots back to ancient Thai practices. As explained by Simon Drogemuller of Orbit Design Studio, the firm behind the building and its interior, 'Kings and royal families would dine this way' – a reference to guests reclining on cushions and being treated to luxurious nibbles by flights of attendants. But while the concept has travelled around the world and now come home to roost in Bangkok, the execution of the building and its interior was done in a strictly international style.

In Drogemuller's words, 'It's not really meant to have a Thai influence or a Thai flavour. Sitting in Bed, you could be anywhere in the world.' Bed makes a bold visual statement even from several blocks away. 'The basic form needed to be something easily recognised,' says Drogemuller, 'so that the building could, in essence, act as its own signage.' Orbit created a hovering tube shape, both visually arresting and affordable to build, fitted with a steel rib system and concrete slab floors to house the programming inside. The volume perches at a slight angle to the perpendicular above the site. The tough, industrial materials and corresponding feel of the exterior carry

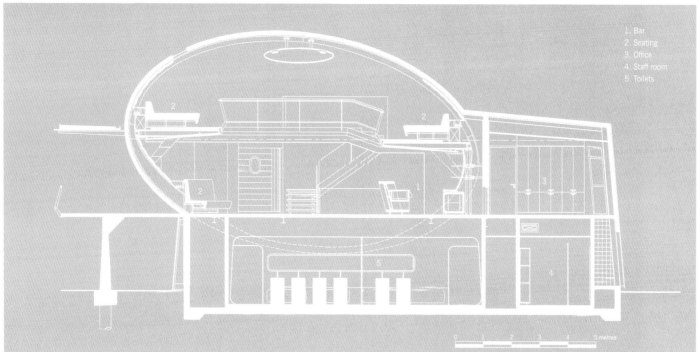

1. Bar
2. Seating
3. Office
4. Staff room
5. Toilets

Previous page: Simon Drogemuller, one of the designers behind Bed, calls the impressive view from the entrance into the restaurant the building's 'money shot'. Top left: In the entrance area, sliding padded-leather doors lead, on the left, to the restaurant and, on the right, to the club. Top right: An array of shifting lights bathes the restaurant's all-white interior in vivid hues.

Bed makes a bold visual statement even from several blocks away.

The conspicuous hovering tubular shape of the building allows it to 'act as its own signage', says Drogemuller.

through to the interior, though here they are softened with curves and given a luxurious finish. 'I didn't want anything to be too hard edged,' says Drogemuller. 'It all needed to appear quite seamless and interconnected.' The entrance lobby, at the top of the floating concrete staircase leading into the tube, quite literally demonstrates this shift, as the concrete platform curves up and bends over to form the ceiling. Sliding padded doors lead, on the left, to the restaurant and, on the right, to the club. Early proposals to have one continuous space combining restaurant and club were modified to allow the spaces to operate independently. Orbit used the separation as an opportunity to bring distinct, though harmonious, identities to each side. The more dominant restaurant section was given a clean, all-white treatment, while the club, finished in darker greys, has its own music and lighting. The restaurant maintains a sense of exclusivity, even though diners pass through the club to use the toilets downstairs, and a mezzanine above both spaces allows guests to spy on activities below.

Orbit aimed to astound guests even as they stepped into the restaurant. 'The "money shot", as I call it, is the view from the entrance into the restaurant looking at the glass front wall and staircase,' says Drogemuller,

The white restaurant area is in stark contrast to the club, with its darker polished-concrete flooring and its independent lighting and music programmes.

adding that it's this area that 'gets the most wow'. The rest is a canvas of crisp white awash in shifting coloured lights mounted behind the backrests of the restaurant's eponymous beds. 'The white epoxy flooring looks like a puddle of milk across the entire expanse,' Drogemuller continues. 'The beds are all white, with white sheets, white pillows and white vinyl walls behind, padded all the way to the top.'

Both sides share similar materials and forms, but the floor on the club side was replaced with light-grey polished concrete for the sake of practicality and contrast. Low sofas, booths and footstools, all custom-made, were upholstered to match. The toilets below, another high design priority, feature flashing rings of light in the approach (lifted from *2001: A Space Odyssey*) and a smoky glass partition (barely) separating the men's room from the women's. Though the visual elements would be at home in the hippest parts of the Global Village, certain aspects of the experience stem from local custom, believes Orbit designer Ralph Dodd. 'The place where Bed is truly Thai is in the service. There's never a sense that the staff are thinking, 'You're lucky we're here serving you.' Generally, you just lie back, open up and relax.' And while there's certainly an opportunity to see and be seen, Dodd says, the

Top left: 'The place where Bed is truly Thai is in the service,' says Orbit designer Ralph Dodd. 'There's never a sense that the staff are thinking, "You're lucky we're here serving you."' Above left: The darker club side maintains the strong relationship between the hard exterior and the soft interior of the building, but with more of an edge. Above right: Drogemuller cites *2001: A Space Odyssey* as the inspiration for toilets situated in a basement space restricted by steel columns.

relaxed service does away with any status-jockeying: 'Asia has a knack of making you feel special and at ease, and in my view, it's more about making you feel like a pasha, rather than like you're looking at one.'

The space, according to Dodd, is 'not really meant to have a Thai influence or a Thai flavour. Sitting in Bed, you could be anywhere in the world.'

Using decorative prints and masses of chiffon, Khosla Associates craft a princely environment for **Touch**, a 'restobar' in the Indian city of Hyderabad.

Hyderabad and Bangalore: With their booming technology industries and growing ranks of local and foreign millionaires, both cities have assumed the mantle of 'Silicon Valley of India'. Yet in recent years Hyderabad, the capital of the South Indian state Andhra Pradesh, had watched passively as the cultural and aesthetic trappings of this new success – high-end shopping, fine dining and hip nightlife – accumulated in flashier Bangalore. Thanks to ambitious and cosmopolitan locals such as Nagarjuna, however, Hyderabad is slowly building up a bank of its own hot spots, which cater to the increasingly cosmopolitan tastes of the city's arrivistes. A South Indian film star, Nagarjuna

recently launched Touch, a restaurant and bar combo designed by Khosla Associates, the firm behind several of the trendy establishments currently leading the charge in Bangalore.

Excited at the prospect of bringing his nouveau glamour know-how to another city, principal Sandeep Khosla and associate Amaresh Anand dug into the project by working through some of the common pitfalls of restaurant-bar combinations. 'The "restobar" concept has been very popular here, but there are very few that work,' Khosla says. 'They're too smoky, the food is not good, or the spaces are not segregated enough.' The simple fact is that a bar is not

Previous page: For the lounge, Khosla Associates designed tables with built-in steel troughs – water-filled basins filled with floating candles and flower petals. In the background, a silver silk-screened print of the jewels of the wealthy Nizam of Hyderabad gives Touch the right amount, and style, of Indian identity. Top left: A glass wall with translucent curtains divides the restaurant from the lounge and bar areas, keeping the functions separate enough to allow

always the most pleasant environment in which to eat. Khosla offers the example of a Saturday afternoon following a wild Friday night, when, as he puts it, 'the space itself suffers from a hangover'. Khosla's solution physically splits the restaurant and bar functions, giving each separate ventilation and sound systems, while maintaining a visual link between the two. To do this, he inserted a glass dividing wall that cleaves the interior into twin sections of roughly the same size. One houses the restaurant, the other the lounge. The synergy created by bringing restaurant and lounge functions under a single roof is preserved by the visual linkage. The slightly older and more mature

crowd patronizing the restaurant adds panache to the venue, while younger, hipper bar patrons make it feel like a scene. Nagarjuna and partner Preetam Reddy commissioned Khosla to create a white context, believing, as Khosla recounts, that 'people like dressing up and entering a white space, and white is a flattering colour'. Khosla, who imagined a sensuous, engaging atmosphere unlike the cold white associated with minimalist interiors, employed several devices to emphasize what he had in mind. This is most pronounced in the generous use of curtains throughout. Faced with a low grid ceiling, Khosla opted for drapery as a means of integrating the lighting without building in a

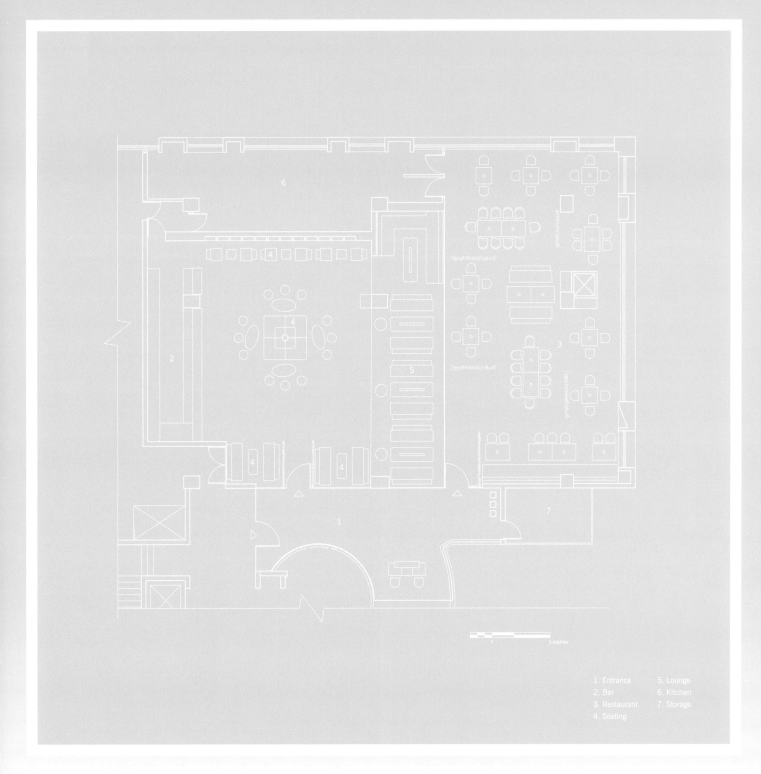

1. Entrance   5. Lounge
2. Bar   6. Kitchen
3. Restaurant   7. Storage
4. Seating

serious diners to enjoy their meals and serious socializers to chat and mingle. The visual link creates synergy between the two spaces. Opposite page, bottom left: Colour-changing lights concealed within the folds of the fabric wash the space in shifting shades of illumination. Opposite page, right: Khosla installed thousands of metres of chiffon curtains between the low ceiling beams: a device for integrating lighting without installing a dropped ceiling.

'We used the low ceiling beams to our advantage, making a design feature out of them.'

Sandeep Khosla

Top: The restaurant features the same ceiling and niche treatment as the lounge, but here the furniture white Panton chairs and marble-topped tables, as well as white Rexine chairs on custom stainless-steel legs is better suited to dining. Bottom left: The round-cornered grid of the ceiling is repeated on the walls in a series of niches. Each niche contains 16 orbs crafted from a moulded resin compound and set against a frosted-acrylic background.

dropped ceiling, which would have produced an even greater sense of confinement. 'We used the low ceiling beams to our advantage, making a design feature out of them,' he says. 'We installed curtains made of thousands of metres of chiffon, which drop from the true ceilings to the beam bottoms. All lighting is concealed within the folds of the fabric. The entire ceiling glows and acts as a unifying element between the restaurant and the lounge bar.' Radiating from the vast expanses of fabric are the shifting saturated colours of a programmed LED lighting system. The rounded grid of the ceiling is repeated in a series of niches that adorn the walls of both areas.

Each niche contains 16 floating orbs fashioned from a moulded resin compound and set against a frosted-acrylic backing. The orbs playfully refract light emitted by LED lamps tucked behind the niches. The round-cornered rectilinear forms of the seating – low and relaxed in the lounge, a little more upright in the restaurant – are canvases for the light show, as well as for the stylish patrons perched upon it. Having completed both lighting and furnishing in such a pure and international style, Khosla felt a 'need to contextualize the space – to acknowledge that this space is within Hyderabad'. He commissioned Tania Khosla of TSK design, his wife's graphic design firm, and

Opposite page, bottom right: In addition to the screen-printed wallpapers, Tania Khosla developed the name and logo for the space, putting an important face to concepts originating in the minds of Sandeep Khosla and his clients.
Above and next spread: In the lounge, one section of curtains hangs lower, producing an area of focus around a central banquette. White curtains and furniture allow for an extremely versatile, constantly changing colour programme.

they in turn proposed silver screen-printed wallpapers featuring abstracted prints of the jewels of the Nizam of Hyderabad, wealthy ruler of India's largest princely estate. At first the clients were sceptical, viewing the designs as possibly too decorative, and hence too traditional, for Touch, but after seeing the prints, they agreed that here was a perfect flourish for a venue embodying not just contemporary design, but the newly refashioned face of India itself.

Savinkin/Kuzmin refer to the design of Moscow's **Coconclub** as a body, an amoeba, a cocoon, a zoomorphic form, an octopus and even a mountain; but whatever it is, it wasn't easy to build.

Sometimes the least likely ideas turn out to be the strongest – certainly true of the winning proposal put forth by the Savinkin/Kuzmin project group, a design that ultimately led to the realization of a venue named for their concept: the Coconclub. The owner, Alexander Rusakov, a banker by trade, invited firms to bid on the creation of an elite restaurant-club in a building originally slated – before the recession – to be private homes. A prime example of what Vladimir Kuzmin, a principal designer at Savinkin/Kuzmin, also known as Pole Design Studio, refers to as 'the Soviet variation of postmodern architecture', the building represented a predicament, as walls and façades had to be left intact. No fans of the style, Savinkin/Kuzmin sketched out a maximum intervention with a minimum effect on the surrounding structure. The team, says Kuzmin, 'put together a new proposal, playing off the symmetry of the building, the square plan and high-tech details. In opposition to these, we imagined an octopus going through the levels of the club. We never thought the client would find it interesting.' After a few discussions about 'Frank Gehry and zoomorphic ideas in architecture', however, not only did the client find the nascent idea interesting, but, to Kuzmin's surprise, 'He became interested in this and *only* this.'

Previous page: Though the architects were prevented from altering the façade of the building housing the Coconclub, Savinkin/Kuzmin's radical intervention is visible from the approach to the club. Above: Glass fins clinging to a wooden construction spiral upwards, forming a staircase that passes through zones of increasing exclusivity on its journey upwards culminating in the VIP area at the top.

'We imagined an octopus going through the levels of the club. We never thought the client would find it interesting.' Vladimir Kuzmin

1. Entrance
2. Bar
3. DJ booth
4. VIP chill-out space
5. Dance floor
6. Toilet

Savinkin/Kuzmin refer to the design feature at various times as a body, an amoeba, a cocoon, a zoomorphic form, an octopus and even a mountain; but whatever it is, it wasn't easy to build. Stretching through the space from the ground floor to the lofty reaches of the first floor, and topped by a self-contained second floor, the cocoon presented a meaty engineering challenge. After numerous refinements, the structural solution ingeniously blended high technology with timeworn craftsmanship. Two models facilitated the work: a three-dimensional digital model that provided the exact measurements of each section and a 1:10 foam model of the body, fashioned slice by slice, that determined the final form. The builders, in turn, made their own 1:1 moulds for cutting the plywood and assembled the pieces, one at a time, to create the walls. Plywood was initially selected as a cost-effective basis for a desired metallic covering, but once the wooden construction had been completed, the team organized a viewing party for several local designers who pleaded for the preservation of the beautiful wooden finish that still graces the interior. Building various functions into the cocoon was less of a challenge, for the only requirement was flexibility. While the owner knew he wanted an exclusive restaurant and club, he had no definitive thoughts on style or

Savinkin/Kuzmin's structure houses several lounge areas. 'It's something like a mountain peppered with caves and suddenly put inside a building with an eclectic façade,' Kuzmin offers.

proportions. As construction progressed, clubs in Moscow continued to sprout up 'like mushrooms after rain', recalls Kuzmin, and with a great deal of success. Following suit, the emphasis at Cocon gradually shifted from dining to clubbing, without relinquishing an air of exclusivity. Within the structure, the revised concept plays out vertically. As Kuzmin explains, 'The environmental "functional zoning" is really based on the idea of levels. As you go to the top, you should find zones that are more prestigious, expansive and unique.'

On the ground floor, the cocoon is perceived more as a set of organically shaped walls than as a body unto itself. It is the most public floor, open to everybody, and eating is the focus. Glass staircases leading to the first floor offer visitors their initial glimpse of the looming body of the cocoon. Drinks and dancing are the agenda on the first floor, where the acoustic folds of the cocoon provide an intimate space for concerts, live music and DJs. Soviet-style 'face control' is the policy for those wishing to enter the VIP chill-out space upstairs, an area used for special events and meetings. Here, too, are the remarkable toilets that are the club's trademark.

The restaurant area, signalled by the presence of red, features glass and metal furniture scattered within and around the cocoon.

Seemingly floating in space – connected to the body of the cocoon by nearly imperceptible Plexiglas walkways – the small pods are fronted by cantilevered doors that are contoured cutaway sections. The toilet pods reproduce, in miniature, the 'absolutely different environmental situation of the cocoon's living wall', says Kuzmin; baffling and strange but sturdy, and somehow familiar, as well.

Hovering in space, the remarkable VIP toilet – the club's coup de grâce – is connected to the cocoon by a narrow glass walkway.

Geomim conjures up the oriental magic of Istanbul's nights on an island in the Bosporus designed to provide '24-hour' entertainment, **buzADA.**

Abandoned factories, arsenals, Gothic churches: these are fantasy building sites for architects and entrepreneurs launching new nightclubs. But to turn an island into a club? Most wouldn't even dare to dream. So when architect Mahmut Anlar's firm Geomim was given the chance to do exactly that, the designer knew it was a once-in-a-lifetime opportunity. 'Actually, I was quite busy at the time, but the proposal to redesign this island, which is the only one in the Bosporus and which was very popular once but almost abandoned recently, is something that an architect cannot easily reject,' he says. 'Moreover, according to the concept to be applied, this place would be the first recreation centre, or rather recreation

island, in the world which operates day and night.' Having served as the Galatasaray Sports Club, the small island already accommodated several sports facilities. But because it had been used only by members of the club and their families in what Anlar calls an 'almost nonprofit, social-club manner' for activities such as backgammon games and wedding parties, it had fallen on hard financial times. 'The place could not be renovated,' recounts Anlar. Eventually, it was sold to a private company, Buz, an entertainment group that has backed several other profitable ventures. Anlar, who had created all but one of Buz's successful venues, was handed the task of transforming the island into

Previous page: The bars and restaurants of the evening section are partially protected overhead by a canopy of matte-white and reflective squares, which take on the hues of the coloured lights below. 'I wanted to catch the magic of the Bosphorus,' says designer Mahmut Anlar of Geomim. Above left: A bar and an open kitchen provide grilled food, salads, pastas and desserts all day long to guests seated at tables with terrific views of the water surrounding the island.

a massive day-and-night complex: buzADA. He didn't have much to work with. 'The place was so old,' says Anlar, 'it was almost like a ruin.' Furthermore, extensive outdoor areas would be required to support buzADA's round-the-clock usage. The crumbling structure was ill-suited for restoration. 'I had to start from scratch,' says Anlar. 'However, the time constraint made it impossible to destroy the existing structure and build a new one. Consequently, I made a plan that lies like a blanket over the existing structure.' Anlar's solution involves leading visitors up stairs to a set of staggered platforms that make up the various functions of the complex. 'In taking people to a higher level, I used the roofs of

existing buildings to obtain open areas of various heights,' explains the designer. 'By doing so, I ensured fast construction and also an architectural identity specific to this place.' His plan produced the desired ambience, and, as he mentions himself, 'the view is perfect'. The facility features two sections: one for day and one for night. A grand swimming pool is the highlight of the daytime area. After dark, guests are treated to a DJ, a dance floor, and several bars and restaurants. They arrive by boat and are routed accordingly by staff at the reception desk. For the pool section, Anlar employed simple colours and forms. 'Embracing an elegant approach at the pool section, I wanted to show

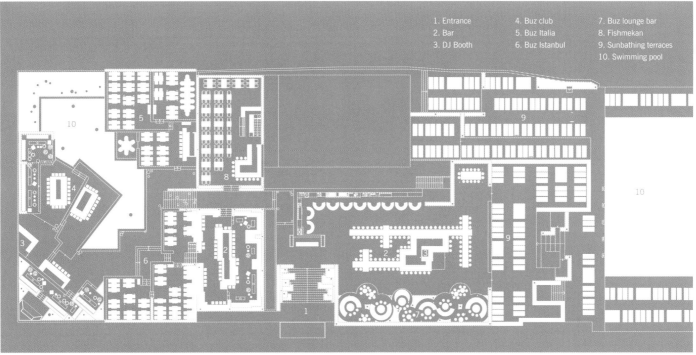

1. Entrance
2. Bar
3. DJ Booth
4. Buz club
5. Buz Italia
6. Buz Istanbul
7. Buz lounge bar
8. Fishmekan
9. Sunbathing terraces
10. Swimming pool

Previous page top and above right: Leaving the bar in the daytime section, visitors discover a swimming pool with views of Europe on one side, Asia on the other. 'The speciality of this 25-by-50-metre pool is that it is filled with filtered sea water,' says Anlar. Top: The buzADA complex inhabits an island, the former home of the Galatasaray Sports Club and a spot accessible only by boat.

'I made a plan that lies like a blanket over the existing structure.' Mahmut Anlar

When the owners and Geomim took over the island, it was in shambles. Geomim made the most of the existing architecture, while realizing the project on a tight schedule. 'In taking people to a higher level, I used the roofs of existing buildings to obtain open areas of various heights,' explains Anlar.

my respect to the unique beauty of the Bosporus,' he says. 'Everything should be tasteful, neat and calm.' To reinforce his concept and to give the daytime area an 'exhilarating look' during the simmering Istanbul summer, he based his palette on white and the natural colours of wood. The evening section has a more glamorous – and conceptual – tone. Here Anlar has managed to interweave 'the oriental magic of the Bosporus', 'the modern approach' inherent to his plan, furnishings inspired by the '70s and 'colours from the tales of Scheherazade'. This translates directly into a flurry of panels overhead, some mirrored and some matte white, which are designed to pick up a fusillade of coloured lights

coming from below; the result is an ethereal feeling of shelter, though the club is largely open to the sky. Anlar believes that, in some respects, the club isn't all that groundbreaking: 'The operational concept is not much different from other places I've seen and created. The only difference might be that buzADA has a broader context, since it is a 24-hour place.' He goes on to contradict himself, however, remarking that the project was destined from the start to be unique. 'There was no chance that this place could resemble any other place I created before,' he concludes. It just goes to prove an old adage: the most important three words in real estate are location, location, location. And this location can't be beat.

Top: Guests arrive by boat and ascend the entry stairs. A welcome desk directs them to either the daytime section, or the evening section, where bars and restaurants swing into action at 7 pm. Above: Geomim combined retro furnishings with more sculptural pieces to create, in Anlar's words, 'the effect of the '70s, when this island was very popular'. Opposite: The club's restaurants, bars and various seating platforms are supported by steel columns,

Anlar's glamorous nightclub interweaves 'the oriental magic of the Bosporus', 'the modern approach' inherent to his plan, furnishings inspired by the '70s and 'colours from the tales of Scheherazade'.

a solution that generates the perception that the sea water below is actually an inland pool. Breaking up the space as such makes for a cosy atmosphere, while also giving guests the opportunity to look at one another. Anlar points out that the 'amphitheatre-like structure provides a perfect view of the scenery', while emphasizing the perfect location: an island in the Bosphorus.

Going underground to create a world-class club, Plazma Studio converted a former Soviet-era bomb shelter in Vilnius into a vibrant venue: **Gravity**.

Before Gravity opened its doors in 2001, says Mindaugas Cukrus, director of PR for the Lithuanian club, club-goers in Vilnius were starved for choice, with only a handful of provincial clubs in town. 'They were playing Eurotrash top forty and Russian hits, catering to Mafia guys with prostitutes and every possible type of person you can imagine in those few Irish-pub-style bars.' But thanks to Plazma Studio and their clients, the Andrejara Group, who joined forces to realize Gravity, Vilnius now boasts a world-class dance club that attracts the cream of the world's DJ crop, including such electronica notables as Orbital, Nightmares On Wax, The Shamen, Ian Pooley,

Marc Almond and Norman Jay. Gravity claims a location that would make any underground club-promoter's mouth water. Quite literally underground, Gravity's home is a Soviet-era bomb shelter beneath a former shoe factory. The entrance, originally the exit of a long evacuation tunnel, is marked by an upright concrete curve bearing the club's name, and little else. 'At the entrance, one finds nothing but a pay point, doormen and a narrow staircase leading down to the 50-metre-long tunnel,' explains Rytis Mikulionis, lead designer for Plazma. The club experience begins in the entrance tunnel, with a suspenseful atmosphere – thanks to a line of fluorescent tubes snaking just

Previous page and top right and left: Gravity occupies the most underground location imaginable: a Soviet-era bomb shelter beneath a former factory. The entrance to the club, marked by an upright concrete curve bearing its name, was originally the exit of a long evacuation tunnel. The 'Gravity experience' begins in the long entrance tunnel, whose suspenseful atmosphere comes courtesy of a line of fluorescent tubes hovering above the floor.

'I was trying to create a light and not-too-overloaded space, which would be a pleasant surprise after walking through a narrow, gloomy underground tunnel.'

Rytis Mikulionis

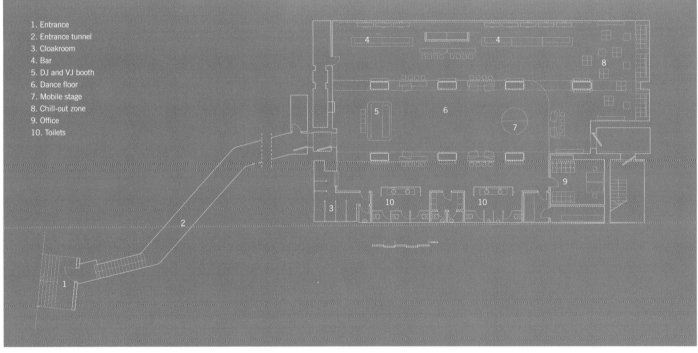

1. Entrance
2. Entrance tunnel
3. Cloakroom
4. Bar
5. DJ and VJ booth
6. Dance floor
7. Mobile stage
8. Chill-out zone
9. Office
10. Toilets

Opposite page, bottom and above: The tunnel is 'the best visiting card for this club', says Plazma designer Rytis Mikulionis. Visitors know they've reached the club proper when they pass two sets of thick vault doors at the entrance to the main space.

above the floor – that seems plucked right out of a spy thriller. 'It's the best visiting card for this club,' says Mikulionis. It also serves a function apart from simply providing access to the club proper. 'People step in here to smoke, to chill, or just hang out. The action takes place between the street and the club.' Two sets of thick vault doors at the end of the tunnel mark the entrance to the club space. The lively club atmosphere is a stark contrast to the cold and foreboding tunnel. As Mikulionis explains, 'I was trying to create a light and not-too-overloaded space, which would be a pleasant surprise after walking through a narrow, gloomy underground tunnel.' The entrance leads to a hallway along the right side of the space formed by the back of the DJ stage. This corridor houses cloakroom and toilets. Bar facilities line the left side of the space, and a centre hall accommodates the dance floor and a chill-out area. Crisp lines and vibrant colours dominate, while flourishes are kept to a minimum. 'The point of the design was simplicity and functionalism, not doing design for the sake of design,' says Mikulionis. 'The main functions are located so that action in the club is constantly revolving – the party is everywhere. Don't be surprised if you meet girls in the men's room.'

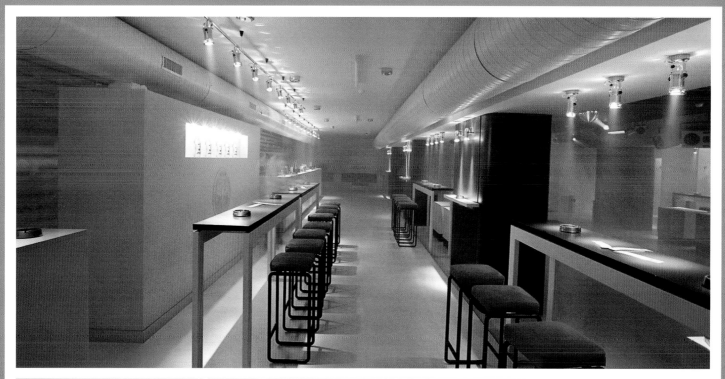

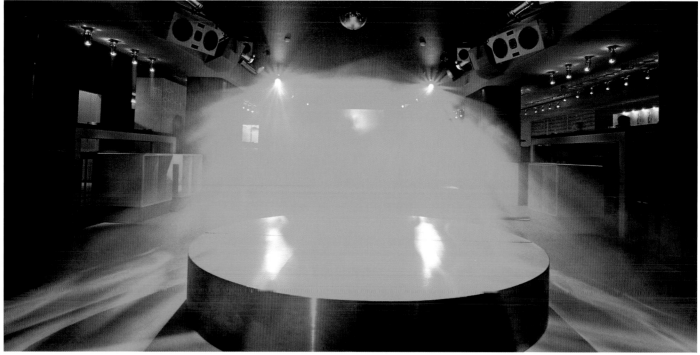

Top: The cheery interior is a welcome reprieve from the bleak subterranean passageway. 'I was trying to create a light and not-too-overloaded space, which would be a pleasant surprise after walking through a narrow, gloomy underground tunnel,' says Mikulionis. Above: The neutral backdrop of the club plays host to intense lighting programmes, especially on the dance floor. 'The main idea was to vary the lighting every night,' says Mikulionis.

Mikulionis describes the look as 'a minimalist interior for minimalist dance music', a club environment with white walls, ceilings and floors contain a smattering of custom furnishings featuring light frames and simple planar surfaces. Furniture is largely white, with dark brown and occasionally red accents. Custom bar-displays are little more than rectangular painted boxes standing upright on thin posts, a construction detail similar to posts in the restrooms, which support circular mirrors behind the sinks.

The vibrant colours that set the tone in this space are courtesy of lighting. As Mikulionis points out, 'Lighting is an essential part of the design. It turns a cold sterile room into a cosy club. The main idea was to vary the lighting every night. One night red is dominant, the next night green, and so on.' Spinning projections and extensively-employed highlight spots add texture and depth. Additional texture is provided by glass partitions clad in translucent patterned films.

These touches provide the club with its only outright ornamentation, and the balance is just right. While Gravity may be the first world-class dance club in Lithuania, both Mikulionis and the owners drew from extensive experience abroad in crafting their solution.

Top: Furnishings were executed in a largely white palette, with black and red accents. Pared-down forms are in keeping with the lightness and simplicity of the space. Above left: Custom-designed drink stands sit on freestanding bases and poles. Translucent glass partitions clad in a patterned film add a touch of decoration to an otherwise unadorned space. Above right: Patterned partitions form a dynamic link between the toilets and the club's main space.

The club experience begins in the entrance tunnel, with a suspenseful atmosphere that seems plucked right out of a spy thriller.

Mikulionis, a club-goer and music lover at heart, describes Gravity's look as 'a minimalist interior for minimalist dance music'.

As any seasoned clubber will tell you, and as Mikulionis so succinctly expresses, the keys to a good night out are 'a free and easy atmosphere, a good mood, dancing and conversation'. In this respect, he believes the design is a success. But the difference between good and great lies in the crafty treatment of details, and Gravity succeeds on that level as well.

Top right: 'The point of the design is simplicity and functionalism, not doing design for the sake of design,' says Mikulionis. Elements like the toilets and the bar, pictured, 'are located so that action in the club is constantly revolving. The party is everywhere.' Above right: Modular custom-upholstered sofas, designed by Mikulionis and partner Evelina Talandzeviciene, furnish a small chill-out area next to the dance floor.

Arranged like tracks on an album, the motley interiors of **Club Tallinn** in Tartu, Estonia, reveal the musical roots of its makers: Kohvi.

Fascinated with international trends in design, art and music, Hannes Praks and Villen Valme, founders of the interior-design and music-production firm Kohvi, list a series of intriguing questions that explain their initial approach to interior design: How can we make interestingly ugly design? How can we create seemingly unprofessional interiors? How can we link design with music? Some of the answers begin to take form in Kohvi's most recent interior hit, the new Club Tallinn in Tartu.

At the outset of the project, Praks drew inspiration from the vibe of the underground club scene in Berlin, where Kohvi's musical pursuits had

frequently taken the young entrepreneurs. 'I saw a solution in the attitude found in Berlin's lo-fi clubs and in the old DDR house clubs,' he says in describing an ambience shaped by 'second-hand sofas and pillows' and 'not much space for dancing and standing around'. Compared with these venues, the typical Estonian dance club looks more like a 'rave club', with wall-to-wall dance floors and bars that give patrons the choice between standing and dancing. 'Some people are surprised to find a club that looks like home.' In this case, however, 'home' is housed in a '70s-era Soviet-bloc student cafeteria. From a distance, glimpses of flashing lights and moving bodies spill

Previous page: The dance floor of the main room, flanked by a bar and lounge area, lures headline DJs like Roni Size to this Estonian club. Above: The podium in the A Room lounge, as well as custom furniture in this space, are lit from below to create a look that is 'somehow not mysterious but cosy', says Kohvi designer Hannes Praks, who adds, 'Lights are hidden behind corners, not in the usual spots. We searched for as many different and interesting points as possible.'

out through tall windows on one side of the structure. Entering, the visitor encounters the Fluffer, a gimmicky construction consisting of a glass box stretching to the ceiling and filled with feathers that are propelled upwards with gusts of air before settling again at the bottom. A feature like the Fluffer might seem to fall into the 'bells and whistles' category, but it is an important component in Kohvi's concept of populating the space with active elements that conspire to make the club feel full even on a slow night. Other 'tricks', as Praks calls them, include rotating light boxes on the ceiling, televisions set into the floor and covered with glass, revolving lampshades and sensor-

triggered jungle sounds emanating from speakers in lavatory walls.

Visitors enter directly onto the main dance floor, which is presided over by a cylindrical DJ booth. Patrons looking for more socializing and less grooving cross the dance floor and pass a stand of textile-clad columns that suggest birch trees and a curving concrete basin filled with rocks and moving water to reach the Forest Lounge. The Forest Lounge combines patterned fabrics and wallpapers, trees, rotating lights and low seating elements to create an absorbing in-between area for chatting, drinking, flirting, hanging out and anything else that doesn't require a surface for gyrating to the beat.

Left: The lounge of the B Room has a printed woodland backdrop (by Estonian photographer Peter Laurits), replete with close-up images of dragonflies in flight. Top right: Ceramic-tile floors and textile-clad walls and columns dreamily blur the visitor's sense of place: indoors or surrounded by nature? The eclectic palette of materials and coverings allows for countless combinations and effects. Above right: Boasting a mirrored DJ booth crowned by an

'How can we create seemingly unprofessional interiors? How can we link design with music?' Kohvi

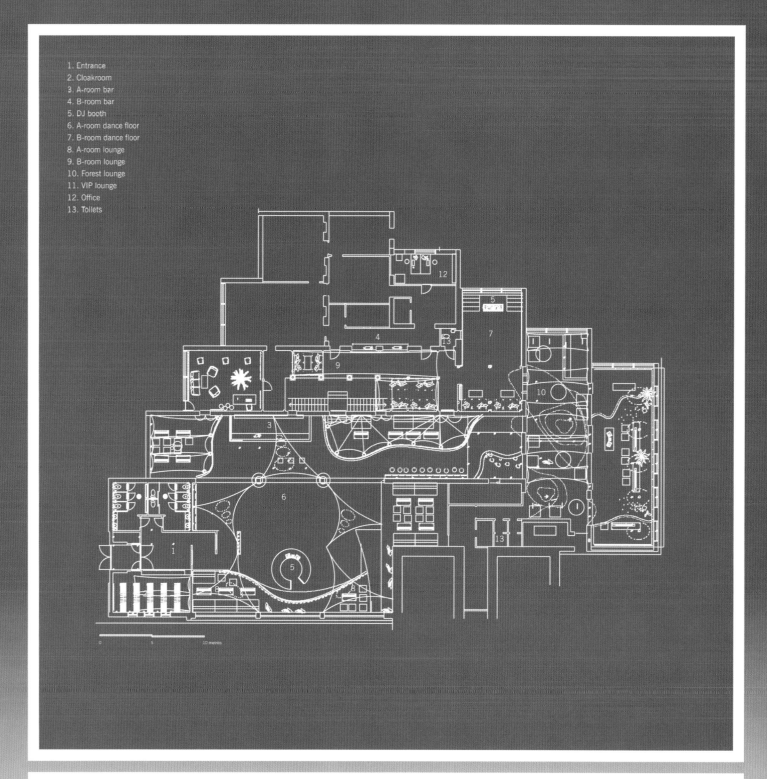

1. Entrance
2. Cloakroom
3. A-room bar
4. B-room bar
5. DJ booth
6. A-room dance floor
7. B-room dance floor
8. A-room lounge
9. B-room lounge
10. Forest lounge
11. VIP lounge
12. Office
13. Toilets

illuminated strip of patterned glass, the B Room – a parqueted dance area with walls panelled in white leather – might best be described as a futuristic adaptation of what Praks envisions as 'the interior of a vintage American car'.
Opposite page, top: The B Room bar caters to guests headed to the lounges upstairs, as well as to those soon to return to the dance floor. Opposite page, bottom left: The Forest Lounge – a fusion of patterned fabrics and wallpapers,

'Estonia is a weird country. Everything is so small, and totally strange things do happen.' Press release for a Kohvi single

trees, rotating lights and low seating elements – is an absorbing in-between area for chatting, drinking, flirting, hanging out and anything else that doesn't require a surface for gyrating to the beat. Bottom right: On the B-side of the club, stairs lead to a narrow walkway between a string of curtained-off lounge areas, where patterned fabrics commune with larger sculptural seating and smaller sofa elements.

Following a music-album metaphor, the club consists of several 'tracks' (lounges differing in design and feeling) organized by Kohvi into an 'A-side' and a 'B-side'. Accessible from the Forest Lounge, the B-side is anchored by the B Room, a smaller dance area with a parquet floor and walls panelled in white leather. Boasting a mirrored DJ booth crowned by an illuminated strip of patterned glass, the B Room possesses a difficult-to-place aesthetic that might be described as a futuristic adaptation of what Praks envisions as 'the interior of a vintage American car'.

Continuing along the B-side of the club and up the stairs to the first floor is a string of lounge areas surrounded by curtains – spaces that combine various fabrics with larger sculptural seating and smaller sofa elements. And then there's the Cave, a tiny 5-square-metre room with a 160-centimetre-high ceiling: visitors looking for even more intimacy can vie for a spot on the floor. The Cave accommodates no more than ten people in prone positions. Although the client did not explicitly request a cave in his new club, Praks reports that he 'knew he didn't want a modernistic, minimalist thing with stone and metal, like an airport. A cold interior looks empty even when people are in it.' Everyone involved wanted an interior that would be 'soft' and 'more

According to Praks, Kohvi created the 3-metre-wide circular sofa in the main second-floor lounge as an icebreaker, reasoning that a bashful Estonian might find it easier to talk to a stranger if they're seated on the same sofa. As the evening wanes into the wee hours, he says it's common to find guests 'lying together on the sofa, like one big family'.

about talk and stories'. Kohvi's anecdotal, instinctive approach – so unlike design couched squarely in the trends or language of the interior-design industry – arises from the duo's music-related activities. Praks, who sees a solid connection between the two areas of expertise, says that music acts as 'a sensor for what's going on in the world'.

Proving that ice has a function beyond chilling cocktails, Arne Bergh and Åke Larsson have created the **ABSOLUT ICEBAR** in Jukkasjärvi from this enchanting gift of nature.

Each winter, several thousand guests decamp to the frozen Arctic and the splendour of the glistening Icehotel, whose entire structure is re-created annually from sparkling bricks of clear ice cut from the Torne River. In the words of Agnetha Lund, who directs the expansion of the ABSOLUT ICEBAR concept, the 'journey from the metropolis to the winterland of the north' ends in the tiny village of Jukkasjärvi in the northernmost regions of Sweden. Since its inception in the early 1990s, the Icehotel has grown substantially, from a 50-square-metre exhibition hall to a space over 5000 square metres that houses a full-service hotel, a theatre and a lounge known as the ABSOLUT ICEBAR.

And thanks to a partnership with ABSOLUT, Icehotel's 'frozen architecture' concept is being made available to less intrepid travellers. Milan and Stockholm have already welcomed new ABSOLUT ICEBARs, and expansion to several other metropolitan cities is in the works.
Introduced to the Icehotel in 1993, the first icebar found its loyal partner within a year, when marketing mavens at ABSOLUT were quick to note a considerable overlap between the two brands. Both pride themselves on beginning with the purest of ingredients culled from local sources, and both blend tradition with an uncompromising eye for the best in design.

Previous page: Guests enter the ABSOLUT ICEBAR through a door of clear ice shaped like the vodka brand's signature bottle. Inside, walls made of 'snice,' designer Arne Bergh's term for the ultra-strong mixture of snow and ice, frame the austere interior. Above: Bergh and the design team's vision is for as many elements as possible to be cut directly from river ice rather than cast. That includes the more than 500,000 ice glasses ordered from around the world each year.

'We have beautiful river ice with life inside it.
I want to reveal that.' Arne Bergh

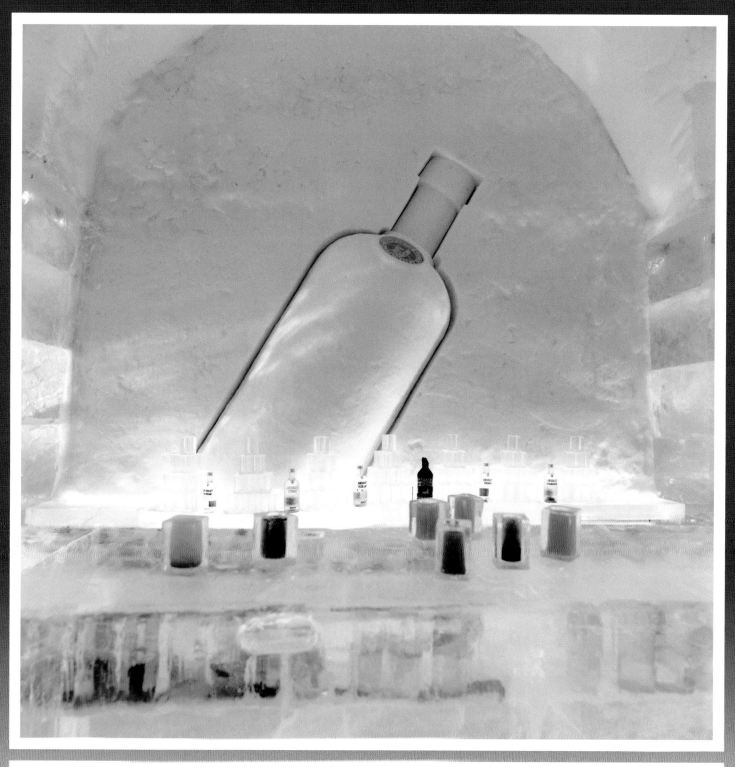

Above: A relief pattern of a giant ABSOLUT bottle adorns the wall behind the bar counter, one of very few elements of pure decoration in the venue.

With respect to the Icehotel, that eye belongs to Arne Bergh and Åke Larsson, who have led the creative charge for the better part of the hotel's history. Neither architects nor interior designers, Bergh and Larsson began as artists involved in early exhibitions at the Icehotel. Both were fascinated by the potential of frozen water in all its guises.

The designers view the melting of the Icehotel each spring as an opportunity to advance their craft with even more ingenious constructions. The latest ABSOLUT ICEBAR at the Icehotel is no exception. Guests enter through a door of clear ice in the form of an ABSOLUT bottle. Inside, they are greeted by two rows of sturdy supporting columns, each a formidable 80-by-80 centimetres in diameter. To the right is a long bar counter. Several tables welcome standing customers, while sofas covered in reindeer hide provide seating. The austere forms of the furniture reflect the duo's reverence for the material. 'I hate to see over-decorated ice,' says Bergh, who disdains the Southeast Asian practice of using coloured lamps and warm lights in fanciful ice constructions. 'We have beautiful river ice with life inside it,' he explains. 'I want to reveal that.' The designers are also purists in terms of harvesting their ice. 'As much as possible, the structure, the furniture, the art, the glasses – everything – should

Furniture and décor in the Icebar are stripped to bare forms, reflecting the designers' reverence for their material. 'I hate to see overdecorated ice,' says Bergh, who disdains the practice in Southeast Asia of using coloured lamps and warm lights in fanciful ice constructions. He prefers to leave the surface of the ice smooth, as though hewn from the river.

be made from solid ice cut out of the river, not cast,' says Bergh. What he describes is no small task, especially considering the production of 500,000 ice glasses required to fill orders pouring in from around the world. The bare-bones rooms of the ABSOLUT ICEBAR, as well as the Icehotel in general, function as a gallery for the sculptures and frozen creations crafted each year by a stable of designers, artists and other creative types invited to contribute their talents to the Icehotel. For the latest ABSOLUT ICEBAR, Bergh designed several musical instruments made of ice – 'real cool' objects that actually produce music. These are displayed on a stage when not being played

in concerts performed by students attending a local music academy. Although the designers must say goodbye to the ABSOLUT ICEBAR at the Icehotel each spring, sister venues in other cities will not be subject to the flux of seasons. That's not to say, however, that the team isn't planning to maintain a steady pace of changes. And the bars won't all be the same. As Bergh explains, the ABSOLUT ICEBARs in other cities will reflect their design-related environments. 'We have a simpler concept in Stockholm, reflecting Scandinavian light,' he says. 'In Milan, there's more of a focus on furniture.' Bergh and Larsson created a new chandelier – lit entirely by LED lamps – for

Bergh and Larsson view the melting of the Icehotel each spring as an opportunity to advance their craft with even more ingenious constructions.

Above: Visitors to the Icehotel know they're in for an unusual treat, says Agnetha Lund. 'Everyone who goes there is excited. They're dressed in capes, boots, and gloves. They can touch everything and they leave the place full of excitement and with smiles on their lips.' Right: The Icehotel also functions as a lab for developing new ideas in ice design and construction. Every year, a stable of designers, artists, and other

the new Milan bar. What the bars will share is an extraordinary difference in what it means to go out for a drink. 'Everyone arrives in a state of excitement,' says Lund. 'Guests are dressed in capes, boots and gloves, eager to touch every surface. They leave the place full of enthusiasm and with smiles on their lips.'

creative types is invited to participate. Their frozen creations are displayed gallery-style in the icebar.

Luxurious surfaces and a focus on sitting, drinking and talking make Vienna's **Club Passage**, designed by Söhne & Partner, a club and not a discotheque.

In the mid-nineteenth century, in a sweeping gesture of utopian democracy, the city of Vienna demolished the medieval walls and fortifications surrounding the old town. Appearing in their place was the Ringstrasse, a carefully planned promenade that invited citizens of all classes to wander among new buildings displaying a variety of appropriate historical styles. Babenberger Passage, a pedestrian underpass beneath the grand Ringstrasse, recently experienced a similar popular makeover. Having decided the underpass was both too expensive and too underused to maintain, the city offered it for development. Recognizing the opportunity afforded by such a prime location, Sunshine

Enterprises – party promoters and record label – snatched up the property and teamed with longtime friends at design firm Söhne & Partner to create the aptly named Babenberger Passage: no longer a thoroughfare, but a destination in itself.

The sophisticated layout and blocky furnishings, covered in a host of high-calibre materials and refined finishes, show no sign of the former life of the space as a municipal tunnel. But Michael Prodinger, who founded Söhne & Partner in collaboration with Guido Trampitsch and Thomas Baertl, points out that much of the underlying skeleton was left untouched. The original four

Previous page: Söhne & Partner refitted a former pedestrian underpass with quality furnishings, like these neutral-coloured leather seating blocks and panels (which can be replaced piecemeal), to create Passage, a smart club for well-heeled Viennese patrons. Above: At street level Söhne installed glass boxes, lit at night to announce the presence of the subterranean space, and added illuminated plastic cylinders, which extend from the street down into the

'Patrons say it's like New York or Paris. When I ask, "Have you been there?", the answer is always, "No, but it's what I imagine it must feel like."' Michael Prodinger

club, 'marking the border between club life inside and city life outside', says Prodinger. Top and above right: After blocking off most of the large staircases leading into the space, Söhne turned them into ramps, which accommodate light columns, while leaving thin strips of stairway accessible to function as emergency exits.

entrances to the passage have been converted into a main entrance, a delivery entrance and two emergency exits. Söhne installed glass boxes at street level, lit at night, to announce the presence of the subterranean space, and added large plastic cylinders with built-in lighting that hang from street-level ceilings into the club. These, says Prodinger, 'mark the border between club life inside and city life outside'. They are visible to clubbers through glass walls that contain all noise within their confines.

The striking triangular lighting was also derived from the original structure – in this case from the engineered ceiling that bears the weight of vehicles passing overhead. Taking advantage of the existing shapes, Söhne used them to house the signature RGB lamps. The light ceiling was an early idea aimed at the primary problem of the interior: its constricting 3-metre height. 'We had to make sure the ceiling wasn't pressing down into the club,' explains Prodinger. A light ceiling, all agreed, would add a sense of volume. Also salvaged from the original structure were several curving walls and a row of niches, which provide the layout with intimate seating areas.

Söhne furnished Babenberger Passage with a flexible system of customized leather benches and tables. Simple forms were chosen, says Prodinger,

Clubbers view light cylinders through 4.5-cm-thick glass walls which, like those used at airports, contain all noise within their confines. Opposite page, top left: In many cases, the designers have given new functions to existing elements, including the triangles in the ceiling and a line of nooks along the back wall, which perfectly accommodate booth seating. Opposite page, top right: The designers added Italian mosaic rounds to the floor to enhance the

because of 'so many other forms inside: triangles, oval walls, round mosaics on the floor'. The team finished the furniture (as well as the walls of the niches, employing an intelligent modular-panel system that allows for easy replacement) in light, neutral-coloured leather to better reflect changing colours and projected patterns of light.

The aluminium bars are moveable, apart from a main bar fronting the toilets. These were custom built by a plumber acquaintance. Modular components can be rearranged daily into different environments, a required element of the programme for the rotating roster of promoters throwing parties here. Sleek

finishes continue in the toilets, agleam with tiled floors and golden walls. In the women's toilet, a long lit vanity mirror accompanied by stools offers a place to freshen up and exchange the latest gossip.

The luxurious surfaces and the focus on sitting, drinking and talking make Babenberger Passage a club and not a discotheque, a distinction carefully drawn by Söhne & Partner and Sunshine Enterprises from the outset. According to Prodinger, the venue was a first for Vienna, which has many discotheques but few clubs. He believes patrons feel more international in this space: 'It's really funny – they say it's like New York or Paris. When I ask,

sensation of different areas within a largely open lounge. Above left: Modular aluminium bars built to specification by a plumber acquaintance of Söhne's designers can be rearranged to form different environments – a requirement of the brief. Above right: The striking triangular lighting borrows its form from the structure's original engineered ceiling, which bears the weight of vehicles passing overhead.

"Have you been there?", the answer is always, "No, but it's what I imagine it must feel like."' Babenberger Passage was the first project completed by Söhne & Partner; next up is another club, this time in an abandoned underground tunnel. Theirs is quickly becoming an unusual but tantalizing niche speciality: transforming underground public-transportation facilities into nightspots with international flair.

Furnishing the interior is a flexible, uncomplicated system of customized leather benches and tables. Simple forms are less competitive with other visual elements, says Söhne principal Michael Prodinger, who mentions 'triangles, oval walls and round mosaics on the floor' as the main contenders for visual attention.

The sophisticated layout and blocky furnishings, covered in a host of high-calibre materials and refined finishes, show no sign of the former life of the space as a municipal tunnel.

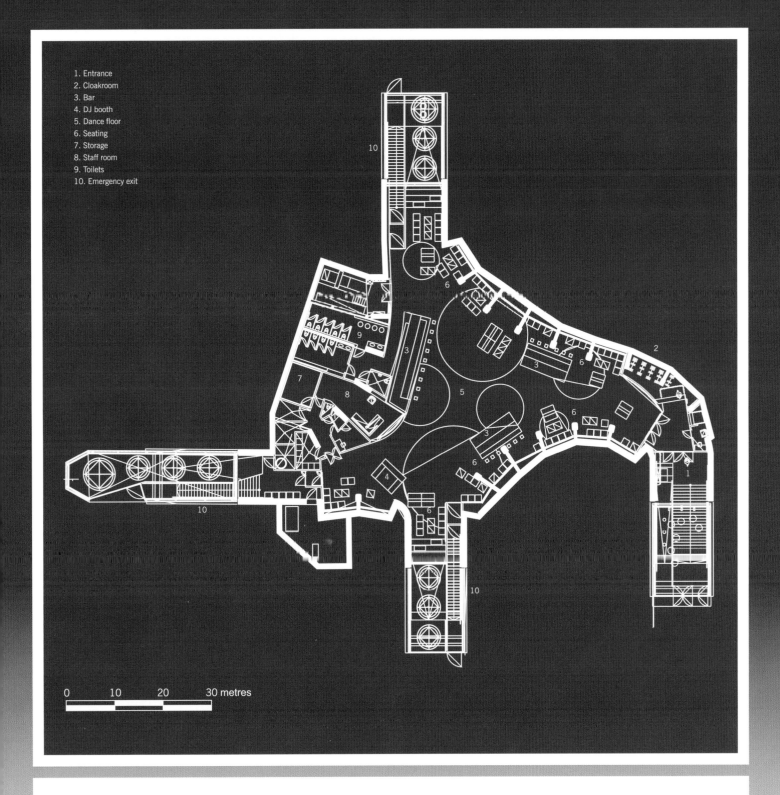

1. Entrance
2. Cloakroom
3. Bar
4. DJ booth
5. Dance floor
6. Seating
7. Storage
8. Staff room
9. Toilets
10. Emergency exit

0   10   20   30 metres

Atelier Kunc telescopes **Club Stromovka** into a sports club of the same name in Prague, adding an original note of curves and lightness to the complex.

On the whole, sports bars aren't known for their architecture. More often domains of dark beer-stained wood, carousing fans and oversized television screens, they tend to be venues whose draw is camaraderie and sport not style. And bars in sports clubs are, generally speaking, an even mangier species. But tucked away in a building next to the tennis courts of Prague's Stromovka sports club is an exception to the rule. Club Stromovka is just as likely to pull in admirers of its handsomely finished interior as it is to attract people who gather to watch the matches in progress. Michal Kunc, who tackled the project along with his design team, Atelier Kunc, credits a visionary client with giving

them room to break the mould. 'The requirement was to create an original and individual design for the club,' says Kunc, 'as well as a practical, multifunctional space where club-goers would feel comfortable.' The brief asked for a club that could stand on its own, rather than a simple adjunct to the rest of the sporting complex.

The interior emerged from a single concept: a separation between the existing architecture and Atelier Kunc's intervention. 'The idea is based on an organic shape made from a natural material, a structure telescoped into the original building,' says Kunc. Atelier Kunc's round-jointed form, made of honey-

Previous page: Atelier Kunc's main contribution to Stromovka was a freestanding architectural structure – a round-jointed, honey-coloured plywood intervention forming floors, walls and ceiling. Top and bottom right: Tables near a bar – made of purposely smashed safety glass and illuminated from behind – are one of several 'functional zones' that Atelier Kunc built into the space. Bottom left: Glass partitions create semi-private niches along one wall of the space.

'The wooden "life form" creates its own environment within the space.' Michal Kunc

Left: A wood terrace at the front of the space that opens onto the grounds of the sports club provides a cosy vantage point for watching tennis matches in progress. Top right: Lining a private lounge at the back of the space are light leather banquettes and square, simple furniture. Bottom right: 'Glass plays an important role' in the design of the space, explains Kunc. 'To optically enlarge the space, we used a series of mirrors.'

coloured plywood, comprises the entire shell – floors, walls and ceiling – of the space. Kunc says the lightness of the wood stands 'in contrast to the grey skeleton, the backbone' of the building. Open at both ends, the rectangular tube does not feel, however, as though it is completely isolated from the rest of the facility.

From the outset, Kunc found it interesting to approach the composition of the space on a macro level. 'I like working not only with the individual parts, but also with the overall space,' he says, revealing the origins of his idea. 'Inside this formerly cold, angular space appears a warm, curved, wooden object

– a wooden "life form" that creates its own environment within the space.' Kunc subdivided his warm wooden world to produce what he calls a 'multifunctional' interior. 'It consists of several zones,' he points out, adding that the primary difference among them lies in levels of privacy. Stools are clustered along a bar made of purposely smashed safety glass, illuminated from behind. Several smaller tables for four, centrally positioned, are joined by five slightly larger tables that fill a series of niches along the wall, each cordoned off from its neighbours by glass partitions whose monochrome-printed surfaces feature close-ups of sports equipment.

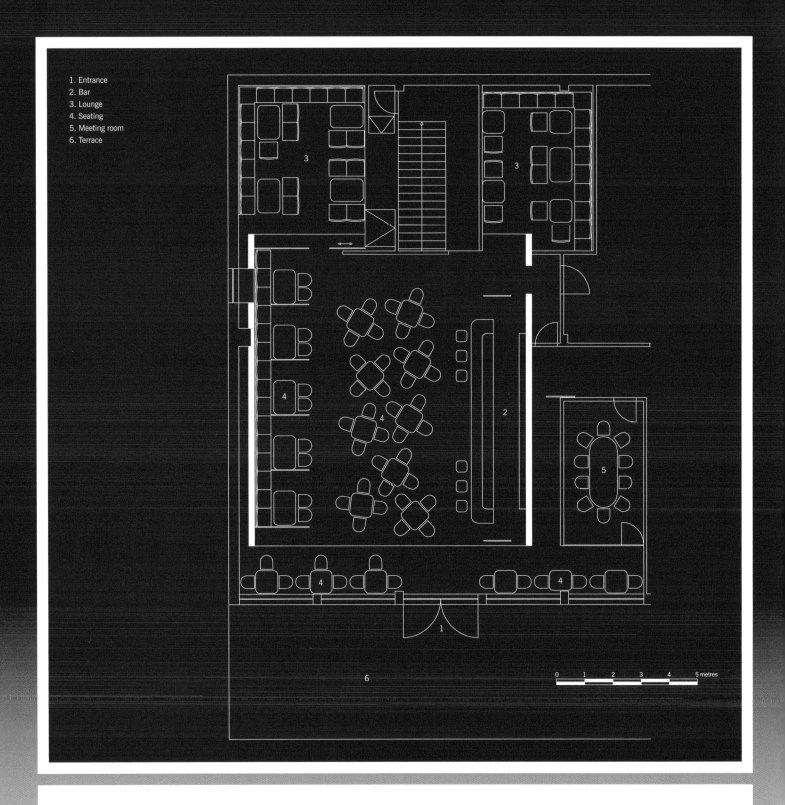

1. Entrance
2. Bar
3. Lounge
4. Seating
5. Meeting room
6. Terrace

Beyond these areas are two private lounges, intimate spaces that Kunc designed 'for business'. Private though they are, the lounges offer their occupants a view of the entire space.

Casual seating characterizes the outdoor café at the front. 'It is connected to the interior through huge windows,' says Kunc, who stresses that light entering these windows 'brightens and warms up the area'. Furniture choices were determined by the smooth curve of the wooden frame. 'Most of the interior details are influenced by oval shapes,' he says. Within the soft and simplified setting, glass elements, not least of which the aforementioned glazed

partitions, make up the better part of the visual adornment. 'The bar appears to be incandescent,' says the designer, also calling attention to the 'dark series of mirrors' used to 'optically enlarge the space'.

Because Club Stromovka accommodates the needs of a wide range of patrons, it appeals to a diverse clientele, including people with no connection to the sports club. 'Club Stromovka is in an isolated spot close to the main part of the city, near the Vltava River,' says Kunc. 'It's a pleasant place for walking and doing sports.' The park in which it is located is referred to as Prague's 'eleventh island', and in the summer it draws scores of visitors to open-air

In another private lounge – this one more orientated towards business meetings and private functions – bright yellow Panton chairs are grouped around a frosted-glass table.

Atelier Kunc's round-jointed form, made of honey-coloured plywood, comprises the entire shell – floors, walls and ceiling – of the space.

Above: The designer emphasizes that Stromovka's private lounges are intimate spaces reserved mainly for business. But large windows keep them visually connected to the main space. Right: Kunc views the insertion as a living organism, comparing it to 'a wood whale'. He mentions the comments of visitors who have said they like 'sitting in this "animal" while listening to music, drinking and having good fun'.

concerts.

Kune believes Stromovka is in harmony with the locale: 'I think that my club is a good option for people who want to spend a nice time together after work, close to the city, surrounded by nature, with good music and food.' Seen as a venue with so many facets, says Kunc, the wooden addition ceases to be a simple piece of architecture. To him it is an 'organism' which comes to life when the patrons arrive, the music plays, the dancing begins and, yes, even when sports are the order of the day.

Goddesses from the world of fine art inspired Fabio Novembre's **Divina**, a Milanese venue that fuses the museum experience with the kick of clubbing.

The name of the nightclub, Divina, was not a revolutionary choice for Milan. In fact, the spot that currently accommodates Fabio Novembre's newly created Divina formerly boasted a nightclub of the very same name. 'It was one of the first discos in Milan,' says Novembre, 'As with boats, it's not so lucky for a disco to change names.' Apart from the moniker, however, the two clubs have nothing in common. The new Divina looks back far beyond the disco era, all the way to Neoclassical times, a period that Novembre finds endlessly fascinating and inspiring.

'Divina is the divine, the divinization of the woman,' explains the designer. 'This term was used in 18th- and 19th-century painting by artists like Velasquez, Cabanel, Ingres and Giorgione, all of whom were moved by the inspirational beauty of women.' Novembre says that Neoclassical paintings of women often referred to 'the Venus', a concept he perceives as 'the perfect inspiration'. In adorning the walls of the nightclub with fleshy images, Novembre hopes to have gone beyond appealing to man's baser instincts to reach a nobler part of the human psyche: 'I wanted to turn the experience of going to a club into the experience of going to a museum. I wanted to give

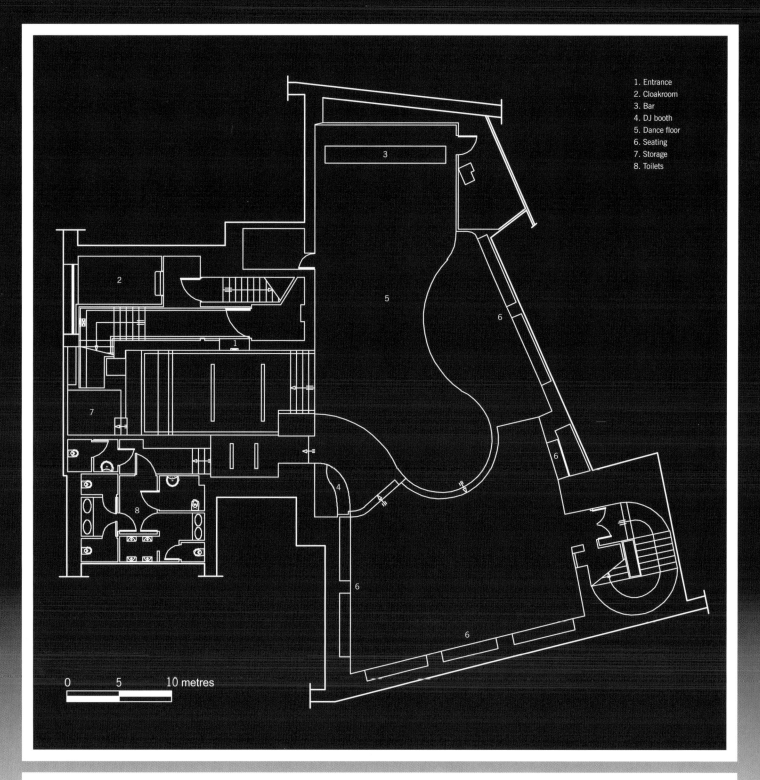

1. Entrance
2. Cloakroom
3. Bar
4. DJ booth
5. Dance floor
6. Seating
7. Storage
8. Toilets

0   5   10 metres

people an art lesson.' Thus the nine paintings that Novembre selected for the club – a collection that includes Velasquez's *The Rokeby Venus,* Ingres's *The Grand Odalisque* and Cabanel's *Birth of Venus* – take centre stage at Divina, whose black walls create a space that is, in essence, a gallery in reverse. Novembre explains that he made the interior black so that people entering the club will be struck immediately by the paintings. This is a museum with a twist, though, as the paintings provide more than superficial decoration. Each is printed on a canvas-like screen of the same type used for large-scale outdoor advertising. Novembre wrapped the material around the back and edges of

recessed nooks that serve as seating elements. Clubbers drawn to a specific painting are logically drawn to the seating that accompanies that work of art. As the designer sees it, each guest undergoes a viewing experience that impacts the entire body. 'You confuse yourself with the artwork,' he says, adding that the act of looking at the picture transcends the merely visual to become 'corporal'. And it is the 'collision' of painting and body upon which he built the whole space. The concept took off immediately, and Novembre recounts that 'instead of reserving a table, a guest might ask, "Can I get Velasquez's *Venus*?"' The most arresting work is also the most prominent.

The dominant red hue of the entrance, with its sensuous velvet drapes, gives way to softer, cooler purple tones. 'From the entrance and the wardrobe, you get closer to the core of the spirit of the space,' says Novembre.

'I wanted to turn the experience of going to a club into the experience of going to a museum.' Fabio Novembre

Top left: At Divina, Novembre's pièce de résistance is a larger-than-life version of Courbet's *L'Origine du Monde*, a work translated, with the help of Bisazza, into a vaulted mosaic ceiling. Top right: The purpose-designed glass mosaic at the centre of the dance floor glows as the heart of the space. 'It's darker on the perimeter and lighter in the centre,' says Novembre. 'It has a strong reflection spreading all around.' Above left: A mirrored form of

Fantasy is the essence of entertainment.

meandering waves gently guiding guests into the club forms the dropped ceiling in the entrance hall. Opposite page, above right: Purple Bisazza mosaic not only covers the walls, but also dresses up the floors, where thin strips are inlaid between more utilitarian tiles. This page: By building the space on several levels, the designer has given guests different vantage points from which to admire the art, not to mention one another.

Novembre worked with Bisazza to translate Courbet's *L'Origine du Monde* into a super-sized mosaic, that lines the arched ceiling above the main bar. It is displayed, says Novembre, 'in a position that quenches the thirst of dancing visitors'. One might worry that all this attention to women would be off-putting to female guests, but Novembre jokes that it isn't: 'The women like the paintings, too. They think, "I feel so skinny compared with these women... I look better than that!"' Matching the curvaceous figures in the pictures are rounded, flowing shapes and surfaces. From the entrance corridor, a sinuous mirrored form undulates down the length of the ceiling, gently encouraging

visitors to enter the club. Inside, lighting tucked behind dark, wavy, decorative elements illuminates the mosaic walls.

In the main space, the dance floor is ringed with curving sections that create different levels. Novembre, who finds various visual levels crucial to this type of space, says, 'You have to have different levels for people to watch and be watched.' Here at Divina, a number of levels also ensures that paintings are high enough to escape being obscured by patrons standing in front of them. Above the dance floor looms a massive hemisphere: a wildly oversized mirror ball. 'The only reference to a disco,' says Novembre, 'is the planet shape

A massive mirrored hemisphere peeks out from the ceiling above the dance floor. Suggesting a planet-sized disco ball, it assumes the exaggerated proportions of Novembre's fantasy land.

hanging from ceiling. Just ask anyone what makes a disco, and they'll tell you it's a mirrored ball.' And in Novembre's world, it's only natural to find a ball with fantastical proportions. Because, as this designer is quick to note, fantasy is the essence of entertainment. In planning a club interior, he says, 'you need to break through the boredom of the working day. You go to a club to dream about new things, new experiences.' It's been a major objective of Novembre's, ever since he entered the realm of club design, to provide users with 'a sense of astonishment and wonder'.

Printed on canvas screens are several odalisques by masters such as Velasquez, Ingres and Cabanel; wrapped around nooks, these screens form the club's unusual seating. 'You confuse yourself with the artwork,' says Novembre.

A new organism comes to life in Frankfurt: **CocoonClub**, the latest manifestation of 3deluxe's fascination for biology.

Underlying the mix of projects that make up the portfolio of 3deluxe – which includes everything from corporate identity and media stagings to works unfettered by the constraints of reality – is an unusual interest in biology. 'We are fascinated by the principles of nature, especially by the idea that objects created by man could adopt the abilities of living organisms,' says Dieter Brell, who supervises 3deluxe, along with Nik Schweiger, Andreas Lauhoff and Stephan Lauhoff. The group first hinted at the implications for social settings of architecture that grows and changes on its own in *scape*, an installation they created for Hanover's Expo 2000. Serendipitously, Germany's

superstar DJ Sven Väth saw the installation at a seminal moment while planning to launch his own club. Two years later Väth asked 3deluxe to take on his new project, CocoonClub, a state-of-the-art nightlife complex that fuses a top-notch techno club with two concept restaurants in a single venue. With Väth's enthusiastic guidance, the 3deluxe team unleashed the potential of their organic architecture in the new interior. 'The initial thought for the CocoonClub design was the metabolism of a cell,' says Schweiger. 'We wanted to create areas with varying atmospheres that would appeal to a diverse audience and would enable different activities – like eating, drinking, talking,

Previous page: In the InBetween Lounge, hand-painted, cherry-blossom motif in shades of pink and purple covers walls, floor and furnishings. The ethereal lighting comes from blue-glass cases containing cold-cathode tubes. Top and above right: A grid of fibreglass rods extending from the ceiling of the Micro ClubRestaurant picks up projected images, filling the space with shimmering slivers of coloured light. Blown-glass lighting objects create a soft atmospheric glow in the Micro ClubRestaurant.

lounging and dancing – to take place at the same time.' To give structure to the concept, the team imagined analogies between the different areas in the nightclub component of CocoonClub and the organelles comprising a cell. At the heart of the space, Schweiger explains, 'The Main Floor metaphorically resembles the interior of the cell, with the DJ pulpit as its nucleus.' Brell concurs, adding that it's 'definitely the eye-catcher in this room'. The amoeba-like structure features a Styrofoam base over a supporting steel construction, with a special ceramic-composite surface that was applied by hand on site. The DJ pulpit is connected by several pseudopods to the Membrane Wall

surrounding the dance floor. The intriguingly porous wall separating the dance floor from the so-called InBetween zone is formed by two layers of custom-designed modular flowstone concrete tiles. 'The Membrane Wall is, as its name suggests, a semipermeable envelope,' says Mareike Reusch, interior architect and press officer for 3deluxe. 'So the centre of the Club is more active and concentrated, while the areas beyond the Membrane Wall are a lot quieter.' To bring the wall to life, 3deluxe installed a projection system that perfectly maps a 360-degree image to the surface of the Membrane Wall facing the dance floor. Speckling the Membrane Wall at varying heights are several

Top and above: Several Cocoons tucked into the Membrane Wall offer privacy while doubling as windows between the dance floor and the InBetween zone. Forming the nucleus of the CocoonClub is the impressive DJ pulpit; the amoebic structure, with its ceramic-composite surface covering a Styrofoam-and-steel frame, is linked to the surrounding Membrane Wall by means of several pseudo pods.

To give structure to the concept, the team imagined analogies between the different areas in the nightclub component of CocoonClub and the organelles comprising a cell.

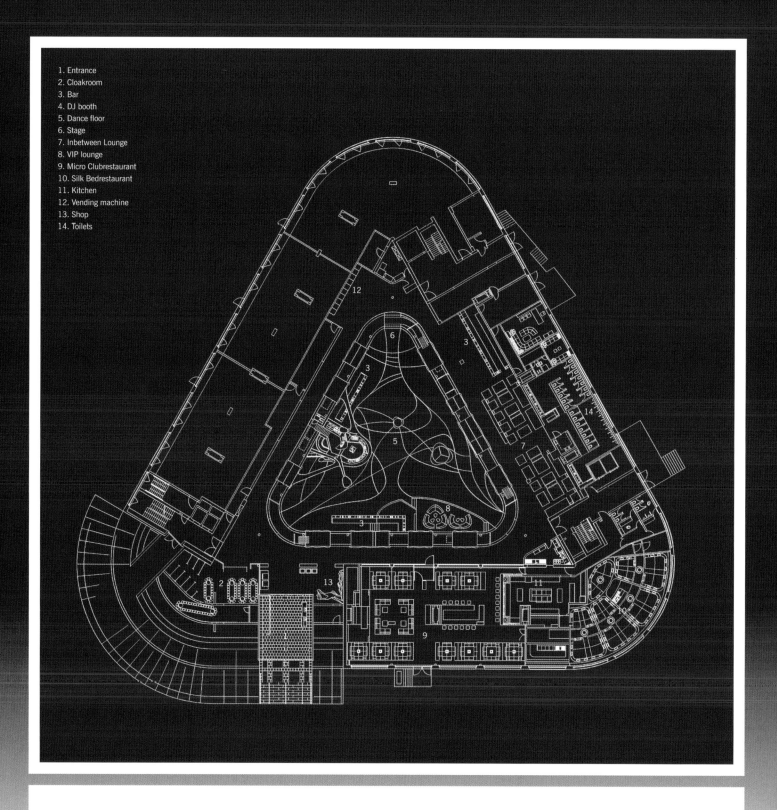

1. Entrance
2. Cloakroom
3. Bar
4. DJ booth
5. Dance floor
6. Stage
7. Inbetween Lounge
8. VIP lounge
9. Micro Clubrestaurant
10. Silk Bedrestaurant
11. Kitchen
12. Vending machine
13. Shop
14. Toilets

private bubbles. These 'micro-rooms', as 3deluxe refers to them, are the club's eponymous Cocoons. Three Cocoons, designated as VipCocoons, are more private, enclosed on both sides by glass panes. These deluxe versions can be booked for an evening. Visitors find the select spaces supplied with minibars, dimmable lights and adjustable sound systems. VipCocoon touch screens allow occupants to view video images of various parts of the Club and to activate a number of service functions, a rare instance in nightclubbing that gives visitors extensive control over their immediate environment. In contrast to the high-energy, fluctuating dance floor and the quiet isolation of the

Cocoons, the nearby InBetween Lounge affords a more open, low-key environment in which to relax. 'The walls, the floor and the furniture are completely covered in a hand-painted, cherry-blossom motif in shades of pink and purple,' says Reusch. Cold light pouring from cathode-ray tubes, enclosed in decorative blue-glass cases, puts an edge on the otherwise tranquil atmosphere marked by soft colours.

From the Cocoons to the restaurants, the space is carved into portions that encourage surprisingly intimate human encounters.

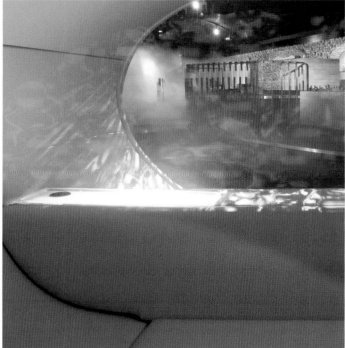

The unique Cocoons – or 'micro-rooms', as 3deluxe calls them – provide customizable environments that are quiet yet not detached from the action and the rest of the crowd. Three of them, the so-called VipCocoons, are supplied with minibars, dimmable lights, adjustable sound systems and touch screens, which invite occupants to view video images of various parts of the club and to activate a number of service functions

'The initial thought for the CocoonClub design was the metabolism of a cell.' Nik Schweiger

Enlivening the Membrane Wall is a seamless, 360-degree projection system that is controlled by a Room Jockey (RJ) who shares the podium with the DJ. With its endless potential for light- and sound-scapes, CocoonClub is like an instrument waiting to be played by an expert musician – in this case, the recital is in the hands of a DJ and an RJ.

The need for a sense of privacy, essential to 3deluxe, was drawn from experience, says Brell. 'Most of our team members are longtime club-goers. We all prefer smaller, more personal clubs. So it was an important design aspect to lend the CocoonClub a familiar touch.' The 3deluxe group believes in putting something of their inner feelings into a project. 'Being personally concerned always adds a positive emotional touch to your design, which is intuitively grasped by recipients.' The ability to develop this type of relationship with guests is yet another way in which 3deluxe's organic architecture takes on a life of its own.

Holzer Kobler makes a night out at Basel's **BarRouge** an experience focused on seduction, scenery and sensuously scarlet surroundings.

Occupying the highest floors of Switzerland's tallest building, BarRouge commands some of the finest aerial views of the country outside of the Alps, offering sweeping vistas of Basel sprawling out below. But while spectacular views may be what draws visitors to the bar, Tristan Kobler, a principal designer for Holzer Kobler, the firm that created BarRouge, doesn't believe that great scenery is enough to keep them coming back. 'Once you've been there five or ten times, you know the view,' he says. Instead, BarRouge tries to make its patrons the centre of attention. It's 'a bar of seduction', says Kobler, who hopes that guests are 'concentrating on the other people'.

BarRouge – and the concept of seduction – first appeared at Switzerland's Expo.02. That first bar, which proved to be a success, featured the same crimson colour scheme and the same focus on matchmaking that characterises BarRouge. The lighting and custom fibreglass furniture – not to mention the effectively forced mingling – were a hit with critics and press. After their successful run at the exposition, the owners were not yet ready to say goodbye to the venture. They relocated to Basel, where they re-created and expanded their concept on the two top floors of Morger & Degelo's sober stock-exchange tower.

Previous page: True to its name, BarRouge offers a pulse-raising sea of red in an interior intended to generate friction between patrons. The concept originated with a bar that Holzer Kobler developed for Switzerland's Expo.02.

Above: 'Narrow passageways in the artificial leather-padded furniture force guests to disturb each other in order to pass through,' says designer Tristan Kobler, explaining a design strategy that plants the seeds for interaction between strangers.

The human scenery and surrounding views are practically the only things in the bar that don't conform to the 'strictly red' colour policy – and it's this very incongruity that makes them the centre of attention.

The double-sided bar is a device intended to keep guests' attention locked within the bar and on one another, rather than allowing their eyes to drift to the windows and the stunning views of Basel outside.

Red carpet in the lobby and a red-lined lift hint at the immersion in red to follow upon the visitor's arrival at the 31st floor. 'Everything is red upstairs,' says Kobler. When he says everything, he means everything: walls, ceilings, epoxy-resin flooring, furniture and lighting – all red. The bar's human scenery and the surrounding views visible through the windows are practically the only things that don't conform to the strict colour policy – and it is this very incongruity that makes them the centre of attention. 'We didn't want televisions or something else like that in the bar,' says Kobler. 'The only things that move are the people.'

Instead, the team devised clever ways to add a healthy bit of friction to what Kobler refers to as 'the game between different people'. 'It's a social thing, a bar – and that determines a lot of the forms as well,' he explains. The seating is one such form determined by its social function. The padded landscape of artificial leather has been designed to seat six to eight people in little clusters, thereby blending together smaller groups. Passageways are so narrow that patrons must stand to allow others to pass on their way to be seated. 'You have to disturb people in order to get through,' says Kobler. This automatically breaks down barriers, ensuring contact and talk even for the shyest guests.

Although Holzer Kobler used the same 'inconvenient' seating for the dance floor downstairs, and although the floor-to-ceiling windows here present the same great views, the environment is totally different. 'Everything is red upstairs; everything is blue downstairs,' says Kobler. 'They're opposite colours, and it changes the atmosphere completely.' The hand-painted ceiling design is the work of British artist Tod Hanson.

The double-sided bar – which lacks the customary stand of bottles in the centre – provides clear views of (and an excuse to look at) the line-up of drink-seeking guests on the opposite side.

Downstairs the atmosphere changes. Music is louder, and patrons gyrate on the dance floor. Gone is the feverish red of upstairs, and in its place is a pattern of blues reminiscent of 18th-century tiles. Closer inspection reveals subtle variations from square to square. Holzer Kobler commissioned the hand-painted work from British artist Tod Hanson. The same seating, with narrow passageways and tables for six, makes sure that visitors bump into one another while taking their places along the side – and not just on the dance floor. Holzer Kobler makes no pretence of having designed the space for longevity. The materials may be strong, but the forms were created to permit easy alteration. 'One concept of the space is that it should change. The bar will look different in two years,' says Kobler. According to Kobler, who 'likes things that are always changing', interior design based on potential modification is not merely handy; it makes the space more interesting. The implication is that while you might get used to the views from BarRouge, the interior should always keep you a little on edge.

1. Entrance
2. Bar
3. Lounge
4. VIP Lounge
5. Stairs down to chill out lounge
6. Lift

'We didn't want televisions or something else like that in the bar. The only things that move are the people.' Tristan Kobler

Holzer Kobler's interior stands apart, detached from the space itself, giving BarRouge a temporary feeling. 'This was all part of the plan,' says Kobler: 'I like things that are always changing.'

Displaying a cool combination of colour, lighting, words and furniture, Atelier Oï's three surprisingly different **Lucky Strike Bars** enhance the nightlife of Geneva and Lausanne.

The Swiss design group Atelier Oï has described its process – insofar as it can be said to follow a process – as a 'search for the non-disciplinary'. This search has taken Atelier Oï deep into uncharted territories that have long separated well-defined creative fields such as product design, architecture, graphic design, museography and art. Like a design supercollider, Atelier Oï slams disciplines into one another at high speed and combines the resulting particles into odd, unstable compounds. The outcome? A body of work that is as varied as it is lauded.

The itch to enter the unexplored was what brought Atelier Oï to partner with Fitch, a firm of international brand consultants, on a project expressing the Lucky Strike cigarette brand in a series of unique bars set in a trio of sizzling Swiss nightlife environments. Fitch and Atelier Oï hit the drawing board as a team, generating guidelines for deploying Lucky Strike's colours and typeface in the first bar, La Sip, as well as some unusual concepts for what the space could become. By combining unfamiliar settings, a brand with a rich history and an image of the target group – an engaged, club-going audience – Atelier Oï transformed these beginnings into three distinctive and surprising spaces.

The first Lucky Bar is part of La Sip, a bustling club in Geneva. 'The first floor is a bar with an Indian touch, and the second floor is a dance floor,' says

COOL IT

Previous page: Industrial materials like rubber, concrete and breeze blocks enhance the air-conditioned, meat-locker atmosphere at La Sip, a bustling nightclub in Geneva. Above: 'Raymond Loewy designed the logo. The connection to Loewy and to pop art made it interesting for us to create a link to the history of the brand,' says Dominic Racine of Atelier Oï. Opposite page, top left: When integrating the Lucky Bar into Lausanne's L'Envers,

Dominique Racine, a designer at Atelier Oï. 'We tried to build something between the two.' The team studied the club environment surrounding the 50-square-metre space reserved for the Lucky Bar, looking for elements that might influence their design. 'It's a really noisy place outside,' says Racine, explaining that the team envisioned the bar as a quiet lounge for chatting over drinks.

He mentions that warm nights necessitated the installation of air conditioning. Of course, to describe the Lucky Bar at La Sip as just a serene spot for cooling down would be to miss the point. Atelier Oï made specific references to the chilly ambience by hanging a curtain of plastic strips (like those found in

industrial refrigerators, says Racine) between the seating area and the small bar, and by repeating graphic cues – snowflakes, for example, and messages like 'cool it' and '35° F' – throughout the space. Industrial materials, such as a rubber floor and a concrete bar, enhance the meat-locker effect.

Installing the second Lucky Bar at Le Cercle, a nightclub in Lausanne, was more of a challenge. Because the bar had to be integrated into the existing dance floor, Racine says that 'it was more difficult to use the Lucky Strike guidelines'. The result is a solution more graphic in nature. Highlighting the interior is the DJ booth, framed in front by a large ring encircling the word 'grooooooooove'. The ring shape imitates the circle of the Lucky Strike logo

Atelier Oï used typographic tricks and applied colour to both counters and custom bench seating. Top right: At La Sip, a curtain of plastic strips, like those found in industrial refrigerators, separates the bar and seating areas. Above: The DJ booth at Le Cercle is stashed behind a wall with a large ring set into it, an arresting feature that dominates the dance floor. Lining the inside is the word 'grooooooooove', in the trademark Luck Strike style.

Playing off the Lucky Strike circle, Atelier Oï created foam- and fabric-covered circles that dangle overhead, acting as both visual and acoustic elements.

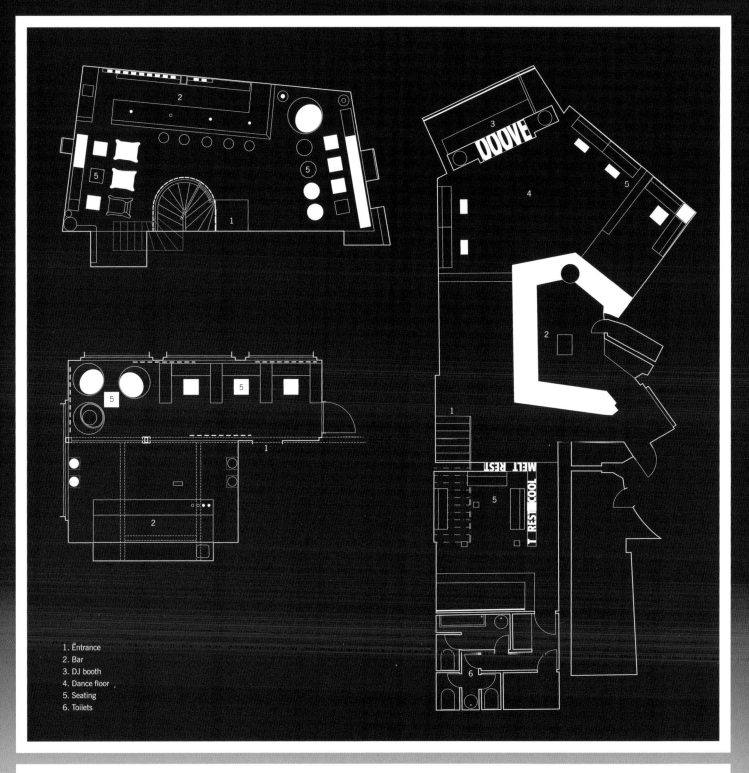

1. Entrance
2. Bar
3. DJ booth
4. Dance floor
5. Seating
6. Toilets

Clockwise from top left: L'Envers, Le Cercle, La Sip.

typographic tricks reappear in the illuminated Plexiglas bar tops. The brand's colours are reflected in custom bench seating and counters.

The third Lucky Bar is in the basement of L'Envers, another Lausanne nightspot. Although designed as a chill-out area, this space bears no resemblance to the bar at La Sip. Instead of a dark, heavy look, the team opted for a light, open atmosphere. Popping out from a primarily white backdrop are Atelier Oï's signature graphics and retro-futuristic furniture. A smattering of foam- and fabric-covered circles dangle overhead. Playing off the Lucky Strike circle, Racine and his team created them to act as both visual and acoustic elements.

While the designers were careful not to repeat themselves from one project to the next, all three venues share a theatricality that arises from a fusion of colour, lighting, furniture and the poetic application of words – ingredients drawn from the way the firm imagined the origins of the brand. 'Raymond Loewy designed the Lucky Strike logo,' says Racine. 'The connection to Loewy and to pop art made it interesting for us to create a link to the history of the brand.' And with their trademark dexterity at genre-pillaging, the designers at Atelier Oï briefly touched on that history before taking it to a completely different place.

Custom bench seating and tables combine with Ball chairs (an Eero Aarnio design for Adelta) to provide much of the colour palette at La Sip.

Top and above left: The graphic treatment at La Sip appears on plastic curtains and walls; a snowflake symbol on the curtains and 'BRRRRR...' on a wall behind the bar refer to the chill-out concept.

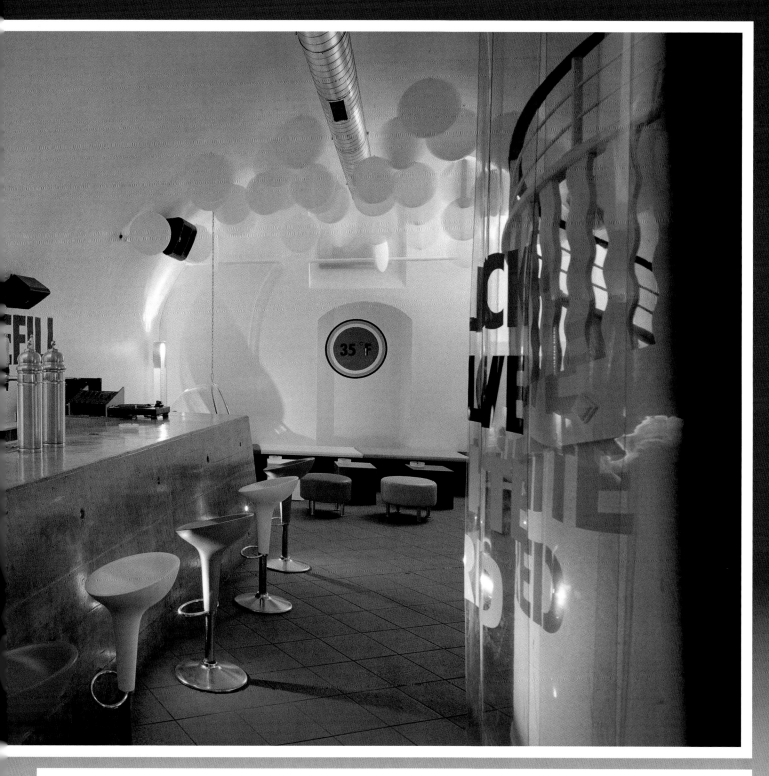

In contrast to its namesakes, the Lucky Bar at L'Envers is light and open. Reflecting the circle of the Lucky Strike logo, foam- and fabric-covered circles dangling from the ceiling are acoustic as well as visual elements.

B.inc furnish Amsterdam nightclub **Jimmy Woo** with a coquettish atmosphere, which does not yield itself up at a single glance, but is revealed slowly and sexily from different angles.

Anyone spending an evening at Jimmy Woo, a swanky Amsterdam nightspot, leaves with a vivid impression of its namesake. Jimmy's bathrobe lies strewn across his fur-covered bed, visible through a strip of one-way glass that allows visitors a peek into his bedroom. In the entrance hall, a series of mixed-media portraits (by the world-renowned tattoo artist Henk Schiffmacher) hang on the wall, causing one to wonder if, in fact, the elusive Mr Woo is among them. 'Jimmy Woo is a middle-aged Hong Kong businessman and traveller with a taste for luxury. He *could* live here; it's his atmosphere,' says Eric Kuster of B.inc interiorstuff, the firm responsible for the design.

After all this, it's disappointing to learn that Jimmy exists only in the imagination. Owner Casper Reinders got the idea for the Woo persona before developing anything else in the club. When he approached B.inc interiorstuff – the creators of Joia, his restaurant across the street – to do the interior, the designers sketched their impressions of how Jimmy's abode might look, and the drawings matched his concept to a T. 'It's really difficult to do an Eastern theme without having it end up looking like a chop-suey palace,' says Kuster. To avoid that effect, Kuster and the team stayed tightly focused on the luxury aspect, abstracting the Asian references into textures and colours, and

Previous page: An etched brass door at the entrance bears an image of a young Asian man, the first of several clues leading to the identity of the club's fictional namesake, Jimmy Woo. Above: A Plexiglas podium, lit from within, stands at the centre of the bar. Here, as elsewhere, the décor balances a few ethnic and period pieces with custom and contemporary touches to suggest an Asian-tinged luxuriousness without looking like, in designer Eric Kuster's words, a 'chop-suey palace'.

'Jimmy Woo is a middle-aged Hong Kong businessman and traveller with a taste for luxury. He *could* live here; it's his atmosphere.' Eric Kuster

Top: B.inc designed the pattern for the black laser-cut MDF screens dividing the seating areas, a motif also applied to the upholstered couches. Each area is completed by black-leather Marac chairs, Prandina lamps and simple, custom-made tables. Above: Translucent curtains, an MDF screen and inward-facing furniture bring an unexpected sense of privacy to the podium, a seating area that otherwise appears to be very much on display.

combining them with decadent and (post-)modern touches. Off the bustling Leidse Square in Amsterdam, Jimmy Woo is fronted by a dark exterior closely guarded by uniformed doormen behind velvet ropes. The chosen ones among wannabe visitors proceed up a staircase, past the Schiffmacher portraits, to the cashier and coat check. To the left, near the rest-room entrances, an orchid sits frozen in a lit Plexiglas case. Continuing through an etched copper door (bearing an image of a young boy that, Kuster explains, could be 'Jimmy Woo as a child'), the visitor arrives at the floor above.

The upper level of the club oozes with opium-den opulence. Patrons gather here while waiting for the dance floor downstairs to open, lounging on period antiques such as a Chinese bed from the 1880s, and enjoying an assortment of the club's signature cocktails. A group of Japanese S/M-themed photographs by Noboyushi Araki adorn the wall above. In the centre, translucent curtains veil a lit-Plexiglas podium mounted by a low-slung antique table, surrounded by low couches. Behind this, and all around the space, stand intricately carved black screens with an Oriental motif. The B.inc team custom designed the pattern, manufactured the screens from black MDF (used throughout

Reflecting Hong Kong in the 1950s, the curving forms of the bar, and those on the wall behind the bar, are rendered in black MDF, chosen because it stays black even when scratched.

because, as Kuster points out, it maintains its black colour even when scratched) and had fabric made to match to cover which covers simple sectional sofas placed along the perimeter. These are paired with black leather Marac chairs, Prandina lamps and simple custom-made tables. Black MDF reappears in both the bar top and the curving shape behind the bar (drawn from fifties-era Hong Kong). Visibility and concealment are the main themes here, with the arrangement of screens, curtains, and light and dark areas ensuring that no matter where one stands in the square room, there is always something – or someone – just out of view. Kuster believes that the coquettish atmosphere,

which does not yield itself up at a single glance but is revealed slowly and from different angles, is what makes the space sexy. Making patrons look good was another priority, achieved in part, he says, by the use of pink-tinged bulbs at the upper level. Where the upstairs is seductive, the downstairs is forthright about its task, which is to provide space for dancing. The dim, subterranean cavern (intentionally designed to feel like an underground club from the '90s) plays host to a range of DJs spinning a range of styles. The highlight, quite literally, is a lighting system made up of 12,000 bulbs that crawl across the entire ceiling and down the walls, creating optical patterns in sync with

Top right: The interior of Jimmy Woo is never fully revealed at a single glance or from a single vantage point. Above right: An orchid suspended in a light box near the toilets is a poignant incarnation of the club's decadent beauty. Next page: A lighting system comprising 12,000 bulbs lines the ceiling and walls of the lower-level dance floor. The lamps are wired into computer-controlled grids that create light patterns into time with the music.

the music: a memorable installation featured in a Heineken ad within weeks of the club's opening. The floor below is a light-coloured wood, which Kuster and team selected because it best conceals the onslaught of high heels and spilled drinks, another smart detail in a club already teeming with smart details.

Ronald Hooft mixed colours, textures and periods to come up with **Sinners**, an Amsterdam club with a stairway to Heaven.

Having studied fine arts and having worked for several years as an exhibiting artist before making the somewhat happenstance transition to interiors, Ronald Hooft has developed an eye and a feel for design, demonstrated in successful projects such as the Amsterdam nightclubs Hotel Arena and Escape. But technical know-how is a different matter altogether, and one might expect a self-taught designer to lack experience with respect to complicated building regulations and insider construction tricks. If his work for Sinners is any indication, however, Hooft's technical expertise easily measures up to his aesthetic grasp of interior design.

The owners of Sinners in Heaven, an established but ailing nightclub near Amsterdam's tourist-trafficked Rembrandt Square, recruited Hooft to bring their club up to standard as well as up to fashion. 'It was like a cave, a grotto-like suburban pizza joint at best,' says Hooft, referring as much to the theme of the space as to the actual jumble of rooms and staircases. And while the interior needed an aesthetic make-over, the primary consideration was some serious work at the skeletal level.
Hooft's first breakthrough was to enclose and build into the small alley dividing the two buildings that contain the club. This allowed for the required

Previous page: The name Sinners put Ronald Hooft in mind of Dante's *Divine Comedy*, which he translated into a ground-floor Hell, a first-floor Purgatory, and a silvery Heaven: the top-floor disco. Hell, pictured here, features fiery red, fake-leather seating and velveteen walls. Above: Hooft designed the balustrade that surrounds Purgatory's void. Integrated into the railing are glazed panels and small, convenient drink rests.

'I played with the concept of Dante's Divine Comedy, with its three levels: a red Hell on the ground floor, a black Purgatory on the first floor and a silvery disco Heaven upstairs.' Ronald Hooft

Above: Purgatory's bar is set in a décor reminiscent of a 19th-century French drawing room finished in black. Framed antique engravings of an erotic nature make this heavenly waiting room a space more sinful than shamefaced.

expansion of the entrance area and provided the space mandated by law for bouncers, metal detectors and cashier. The covered alley also accommodates the new DJ booth and, above that, the housing for an overhauled ventilation system. Moving these out of the pre-existing footprint made room for an expansion of the entry-level dance floor, increasing the occupancy from 300 to 600 people. In accordance with safety regulations, Hooft added two-door bay emergency exits, commandeered the area under the staircase for coat storage, and widened and improved the staircase leading to the upper levels. Another improvement was the conversion of the ground floor's original five bars, which required a staff of ten, to a single bar that runs the length of the ground

floor and functions with a staff of only five. Hooft cut a chunk from the dance floor ceiling to create a mezzanine and installed mirror ceilings above the void, taking the double-height space soaring to what seems to be quadruple-height. Also needed was better soundproofing in the walls that separate the club's spaces from the bedrooms of surrounding neighbours and a residential hotel. Given the location in the old city centre, such considerations were often extremely taxing. 'If someone were to propose starting up a club in this space, I would advise against it. It's too much effort. It's ridiculous,' laughs Hooft. So much physical change was required that one of Hooft's initial recommendations was to drop the club's name, Sinners in Heaven, and start

When club-going sinners finally reach Heaven, they are greeted by cheery walls either painted in candy-coloured stripes or covered in shimmering sequins. Opposite page: Referring to the mix of periods, textures and colours, Hooft calls his style 'tight and cosy'. In designing the nightclub, Hooft sometimes had to fight his urge to fiddle with details. In the context of use, bolder interventions are more important.

from scratch. But the owners had faith in their brand and decided to keep it in a shortened form – Sinners – which gave Hooft the basis for his interior theme. 'I played with the concept of Dante's *Divine Comedy*, with its three levels: a red Hell on the ground floor, a black Purgatory on the first floor and a silvery disco Heaven upstairs.' Thus the fiery red, fake-leather seating and velveteen walls of the ground floor make the transition to a Purgatory suggestive of a 19th-century French drawing room finished in black (though framed erotic engravings make this a naughty Purgatory) and, finally, to a sequin-spangled, second-floor Heaven, with striped candy-coloured wallpaper.

The attention to colour and the mixture of textures and periods is typical of Hooft, who calls the style 'tight and cosy'. He adapts his personal taste and interpretation of fashion to the individual client. In designing a nightclub, he says that the task is 'to make a space attractive for people right now. You can't be too avant-garde; you have to be spot-on in terms of style.' Though Hooft believes that the style of a club interior is unlikely to remain relevant for more than five years, his structural refurbishment of Sinners appears sound enough to last for a decade or more. 'If you take out all the skin elements, you still have a great space, architecturally speaking.'

Next spread: Purgatory is actually a mezzanine level, which embraces a large void above the dance floor down in Hell. A construction of disco balls hangs out over the void, while a mirrored ceiling visually doubles the height of the space.

Regardless of location, each **Supperclub** – a surprising venue currently found in Rome, Amsterdam and in the form of a cruise – relies on a library of designs created by Concrete.

Supine, barefoot diners recline on mattresses furnished with crisp, white linen, nibbling on exotic *amuse-gueules* and drinking champagne, as harlequins on stilts whirl about the room, dancing to a DJ's set, while a wash of multicoloured lights bathes the walls in an ever-changing aurora. It may sound dreamlike (and it is), but it's just business as usual at Amsterdam's Supperclub, which has been serving up equal portions of gourmet treats and fantastical theatre night after night for more than a decade. The history of the club, which precedes the current management group, is all but apocryphal. But as the legend goes, a group of Dutch artists, singers, dancers and writers banded together in the late '80s to create a chimerical combination of catering and theatre, hosting a series of roving events that blended their art with performances and conceptual cooking. In 1994 the group found a permanent shelter on the current site, a former tea room. Audiences that managed to find out about it were treated to evenings of phenomenal creativity, spiced with a substantial element of unpredictability: stories abound of leaky ceilings and chefs that sometimes couldn't be bothered to prepare a meal, instead ordering Happy Meals from McDonald's for the guests. Seeing the potential for the idea, as well as the immense gap in leadership, in 1997 Bert van der Leden,

Previous page: In Supperclub Amsterdam's Salle Neige, diners can eat from silver trays while relaxing on stainless-steel bunk beds that line the walls. The more conventional may opt for the Verner Panton tables and chairs at the centre of the room. Rob Wagemans of Concrete mentions that the room's elephant-drum tables look sturdy enough to hold uninhibited dancers. Above: The Salle Neige at Supperclub Cruise ups the reclining-dining ante by

the current owner, stepped in to put measures in place that have allowed the continued growth and progress of the Supperclub. Van der Leden, a benign dictator who kept most of the original group and encouraged them to carry out their ideas, has seen the Supperclub evolve into one of Holland's hippest (if least definable) brands, with new branches in Rome and on a yacht (the Suppercruise), and several more on the way, not to mention a popular series of compilation CDs and a number of other products. Much of this success can be chalked up to the work of design firm Concrete, hired by Van der Leden in the early days of his tenure to provide a physical stage as solid as the performers

who would be gracing it. Rob Wagemans, one of Concrete's founders, refers to the initial design as 'a white box where artists could do their thing'. He says that he and his team 'tried to materialize temptation' in an attempt 'to get people to do things they wouldn't expect to do'. The goal of performers and artists at the Supperclub goes beyond entertaining a passive audience. They invite guests to participate in the evening's festivities, a concept that Concrete manifested in design elements such as large tables that resemble the sturdy elephant drums featured at the circus: objects that look strong enough to support the weight of people dancing on top of them. Rather than installing toilets labelled

placing up to 76 diners on a single bed. The room combines atmospheric, colour-changing lights with theatre lighting to achieve its dreamy effect. This page: Deep-red flooring and walls, along with red velour curtains, mark the Bar Rouge in Rome. Modelled on the Amsterdam original, the Bar Rouge is part of a 'library' of design archetypes that Concrete plans to use for future Supperclub locations.

Van der Leden, a benign dictator who encouraged
the original group to carry out their ideas,
has made Supperclub a highly hip Dutch brand.

The Salle Neige in Rome duplicates the concept of the Amsterdam location. Computer-controlled lighting, which can be accessed via network from remote locations, ensures a variety of combinations adaptable for different performances.

A series of roving events that blend art with performances and conceptual cooking provided Supperclub with a point of departure.

Before dinner, guests warm up with drinks in Amsterdam's Salon Coloré, the same room that will welcome them later for a night of dancing to the DJ's mix.

'Men' and 'Women', the designers opted for signs marked 'Homo' and 'Hetero'. Lounge elements inside the restrooms encourage patrons to hang out and chat, while portholes ringed with lights, which serve as mirrors above the sinks, are made of one-way glass that permits people standing in the hall to look on as women reapply lipstick and men rework the gel in their hair. These elements fall into what Wagemans refers to as a 'library' of designs, an invaluable source of information for planning new Supperclub interiors. Basic elements are the Salle Neige, a white space that functions as the main dining room; the Toilettes Noires; and the Bar Rouge, a red bar where patrons gather before and after meals, and where dancing often goes on until the wee hours of the morning. While the look is consistent, it varies from location to location. Supperclub Rome, for example, features the Salle Baroque, replete with original finishes and detailing in walls and ceiling; while Suppercruise boasts a seductive Bar Noir and Toilettes Rouge. Regarding upcoming locations in San Francisco and Cape Town, Wagemans simply smiles and says that San Francisco will feature 'the most beautiful disabled toilets the world has ever seen'. Given the ceaseless originality of the existing Supperclub locations, it's not difficult to imagine the team at Concrete living up to this challenge.

A snaking white couch in the Salon Coloré creates booths for more intimate groups within its switchbacks, while a straight banquette lines the other wall. Spots with coloured search lights vary the ambience.

Concrete rejected toilets labelled 'Men' and 'Women' in favour of signs marked 'Homo' and 'Hetero'.

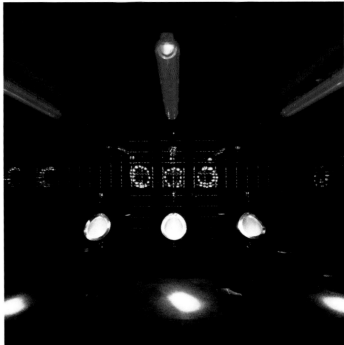

Top right: Pin spots illuminate stainless-steel urinals in toilets with no other lighting. Instead of Men's and Women's, the Supperclub offers guests the choice of Homo or Hetero, removing ordinary modes of thought and challenging inhibitions. Above right: Rob Wagemans and the team from Concrete 'tried to materialize temptation' by piling diners together in the same bed, for example, another attempt 'to get people to do things they wouldn't expect to do'.

Hip and impressive inside and out, **Now & Wow** is Hub's transformation of an old Rotterdam grain silo into a contemporary night club.

'The building had something filmic about it,' says Nyo, recalling her first walk-through of Now & Wow's prospective new location, a grain warehouse on Rotterdam's fabled waterfront. Nyo, a.k.a. Elsbeth van Noppen, designs visuals for the Rotterdam club. The building's first silos were built in 1910, and following waves of additions made by Dutch architectural luminaries, among them Brinkman & Van der Vlugt and Herman Haan, the imposing structure had acquired iconic status. 'It was so huge, so bizarre,' says Nyo. 'So clumsy and yet somehow so beautiful.' In short, the notorious club, which had outgrown its old digs in another warehouse closer to the city centre, had found

the perfect place to serve as its new venue.

Ted Langenbach, Now & Wow's notorious creative director, is unusually sensitive to zeitgeist and its fleeting nature. Langenbach compares Now & Wow to the Palais de Tokyo, an up-to-the-minute Parisian haven for contemporary art and, like the Rotterdam club, a place that makes a tremendous effort to keep its finger on the cultural pulse. 'It's a flow you have to anticipate,' says Langenbach. 'It's ironic, part of a new urban lifestyle.' The buildings – one in Holland, the other in France; two hulking, raw shells housing evanescent carnivals of art, fashion and performance, are structurally

Previous page: More than 5000 bottles were used to construct the sponsorship stacks behind the bars. HUB designer Robbert de Vrieze calls it 'a scale and amount that meshes seamlessly with the silo'. Above: Here HUB used wooden partitions, installed between existing concrete pillars, as projection screens. Newly added concrete slabs – such as this one at the coat-check area – function as counters.

analogous as well. From the start, the Now & Wow team relished the contrast between the shell and its delicately-confected contents. 'The size, scale, and roughness demanded an unusual approach to designing the interior. It was impossible, as well as inappropriate, to make it nice and detailed all the way through,' explains Robbert de Vrieze of HUB, the team charged with the interior design of Now & Wow.

Instead, only a basic infrastructure was put in place. The grain silo was fitted with a few large, simply-constructed walls, as well as extensive lighting, projection and sound systems. Several columns were removed to create two

large rooms. 'The rooms became huge, like cathedrals,' says Langenbach. Concrete bars and counters were put into place for serving drinks and checking coats, and an ingenious routing scheme was devised that provides each of the two main rooms – dubbed Now and Wow – with separate entrances, enabling the club to be rented out piecemeal. There is little in the club that could be described as furniture. Playing off the inherent repetition of the architecture, one example is a numbered series of 'sitting rolls' created by HUB. Based on punching bags, these serpentine rolls can be arranged to provide seating throughout the club. De Vrieze jokes that the resulting 'anti-

Left: The scale and rawness of Now & Wow's interior demanded hefty additions, like this sponsor-related element, with its reference to bulk goods. Top right: The scale of the Now room makes it appropriate for large concerts as well as DJ-orchestrated events. Above right: HUB made a distinction between the materials used to make functional additions to the original architecture (such as counters and walls) and the pieces created for sponsors.

'The size, scale, and roughness demanded an unusual approach to designing the interior.' Robbert de Vrieze

Left: T-shirts, CDs and other merchandise are piled in tall storage bins behind the counter of the kiosk in Superwow. Right: Creative director Ted Langenbach, who calls the club 'part of a new urban lifestyle', sees Now & Wow not only as a venue for music and dancing, but also as a forum for bold forays into experimental fashion, performance, theatre and media art.

lounge' is a counterweight to the prevailing lounge culture, for the construction of the rolls allows for upright sitting only, no reclining.

Apart from these additions, permanent fixtures in the space are few but noteworthy. HUB installed an information point and a shop in Superwow, the central square of the club. Tall glass storage bins are piled high with club merchandise and products promoting the club's sponsors.

HUB used carefully chosen materials to distinguish the more polished work for the sponsor from the rough-hewn interior of the rest of the club. 'The elements of the exterior are rough, non-treated metals, but within the object we used

stainless steel and high-gloss finishes in adherence with the image of this sponsor,' explains De Vrieze. Among the few elements of the permanent interior that incorporate colour are sponsor-related constructions above the bars. Massive illuminated walls of stacked bottles, more than 5000 in total, are another example of repetition, says De Vrieze, 'in a scale and amount that meshes seamlessly with the silo'.

The remainder of the interior provides a backdrop for the club's 'set pieces': temporary installations created by the Now & Wow team based on each week's theatrics. Themes ranging from the vague ('puerility, neo-nihilism'

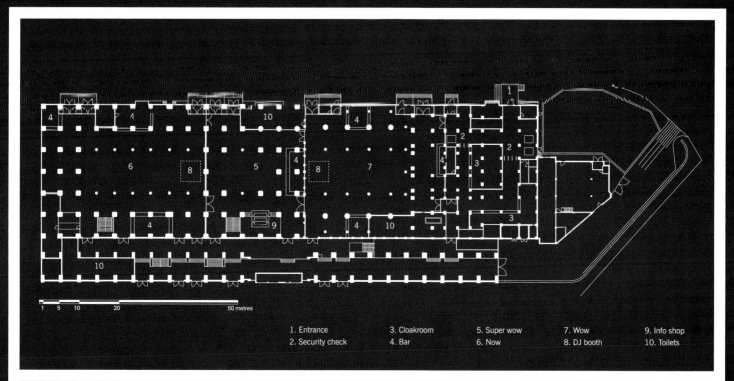

1. Entrance
2. Security check
3. Cloakroom
4. Bar
5. Super wow
6. Now
7. Wow
8. DJ booth
9. Info shop
10. Toilets

Riffing on the repetition inherent to the warehouse architecture, Hub crafted a series of numbered 'sitting rolls' based on punchbags. Grouped together, they form an 'anti-lounge', where guests can sit but not recline.

Hub's 'anti-lounge' is a counterweight to the prevailing lounge culture, for the construction of Now & Wow's 'sitting rolls' requires guests to sit up straight – no reclining.

Above: Regularly spaced columns, ceiling downspouts and the original purpose of the building – to store raw materials – inspired the themes of repetition and bulk visible in many elements, including sponsorship displays consisting of bottles stacked to the ceiling in front of an illuminated wall. Opposite page, top left: The former industrial grain silo is located in Rotterdam's fabled port area. Opposite page, top right and above: Some of the early

offers Langenbach) to the kookily concrete ('Nazi schoolgirls wearing bicycle shorts' remarks De Vrieze) are translated into fleeting convergences of visual imagery, fashion displays and sets; here one weekend, gone the next. The memorable quality of the club stems from the stark contrast between, in Nyo's words, 'the atmosphere of extreme immobility and power, almost of oppression' and something as light and intangible as the circus of images within.

silos, dating back to 1910, still have grain in them. From their very first visit, the designers were enthralled by the sheer scale and unfinished quality of the building, attributes preserved in their conversion. Many of the original silo's downspouts bear the Art-Deco flourishes of famed architects Brinkman & Van der Vlugt, who designed one of many expansions made to the building.

Overlooking the harbour in Ghent, Glenn Sestig's **Culture Club** combines the right crowd and great music in a monumental '80s-redux interior.

Every so often a nightclub stumbles upon a fleeting convergence of the invisible energy lines of fashion, music and style, subsequently assuming legendary status as the centre of a scene. For the electro-clash, '80s-revival movement in Europe, that legendary epicentre must certainly be Ghent's Culture Club. If forced to isolate *the* moment in which the Culture Club achieved that status, one would probably look to October 2002, when Colette of Paris – arguably the most influential fashion boutique in the world – chose the Culture Club as the site of the launch party for its new magazine and collection. For the affair, Colette chartered a special high-speed train to shuttle 400 invitees to an event featuring a number of top musical acts, providing in a single evening enough hype to fuel years of clubland success. It's a serendipitous mix that has propelled the Culture Club beyond simple 'fun night out' status. The club's designer, Glenn Sestig, credits owners and promoters Belmondo for bringing together the right crowd and the best music: 'They really know how to do it.' But the role played by Sestig's cold, spare but engaging design, which seems drawn from the synth lines and crisp rhythms of the music itself, cannot be discounted.

Previous page: Architect Glenn Sestig employed several devices in the Large Room – such as a raised platform, an isolated DJ booth and bar at the centre, and a glassed-off corridor to the left – to create varied visual planes and areas within the rectangular space. Above left: Sestig calls his sense of scale and his use of simple stone and concrete forms 'monumental', adding that 'people like monumentality, and I like to do things that look monumental'.

'I know what it is to go out. You want a good bar and nice toilets, not just a beautiful place.'

Glenn Sestig

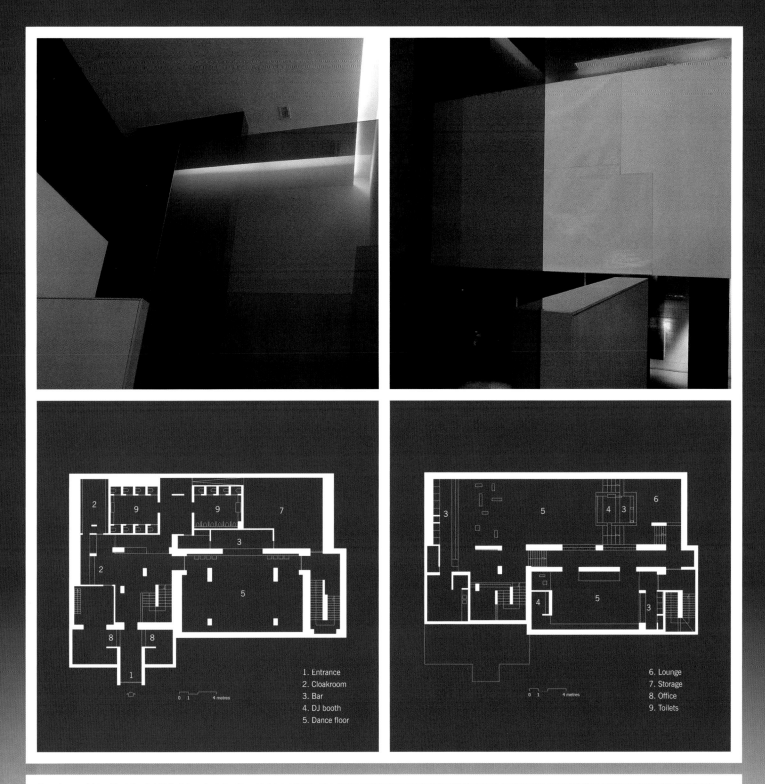

Opposite page, right and top left and right: Sestig's contrast of matte and lustrous materials, not-quite-intersecting planes and jewel-toned lighting seems drawn from the spare synth lines and glamour of the '80s electro-clash music behind the club's rise to fame. Above left: Ground floor. Above Right: First floor.

The recurrence of black-lacquered mirrors, dark glass partitions and thin strips of jewel-coloured lighting feels rooted in the same '80s glamour that marked that decade's fashion and music, but Sestig's application of these elements resists it. Notably, Sestig's trademark use of not-quite-intersecting planes (creating gaps that accommodate recessed indirect lighting) and unexpected pairings of contrasting materials, such as mat Brazilian stone and simple plasterboard, makes the look more '80s redux than '80s revival. Despite the strong visual impact of the design, the functionality of the space is Sestig's greatest accomplishment. In mapping out the programme, he drew on his own experience of elbowing his way through crowded bars and dealing with other dysfunctional spaces: 'I know what it is to go out. You want a good bar and nice toilets, not just a beautiful place.' To achieve the right ambience (and to avoid fighting with the floor plan of the former school in Ghent's harbour-front area, a building that had housed an underground club for years), Sestig and Belmondo opted for a few smaller rooms rather than one big warehouse, rave-style dance floor. 'It's a new party idea, dividing the place into smaller and smaller spaces. That way you see lots of different people in groups together, not just one big visual thing.'

The central corridor provides access, at several places, to both the Large Room and the smaller room on the first floor; it is evidence of Sestig's devotion to functionality and flow, which were every bit as important to the designer as the aesthetics of the club.

The Large Room on the first floor is the focus, a long rectangular space that Sestig visually subdivided using several ingenious formal tricks, such as inserting a higher level at the back to serve as a lounge platform, situating the DJ booth in the centre as a raised island flanked by a bar and adding a section of lowered ceiling towards the other end. Overlooking one side of the Large Room are good-sized windows which line a parallel corridor that leads to a smaller first-floor room, about half the size, with separate DJs and sound system. Downstairs is yet a third room, more recently added; though generally functioning as a chill-out and gathering space, it can be recruited as another dance area on a busy night. Carving several distinct spaces from a larger space can result in a sense of disorientation and a lack of circulation, issues that Sestig addressed in drafting the initial plans. 'The circulation is very important, with many entrances and exits providing the flow,' he says. 'It's exciting to watch someone go into a room, yet not know if you will find them there once you go in.' For the sake of interesting views and the easy movement of patrons from one area to another, he aimed for a sense of spaciousness.

Planar motifs reappear in the toilets in the form of concrete and black-lacquer slabs, but lighting here contrasts with that used in the rest of the club.

The planar language of form achieves remarkably complex effects with the use of simple means. Sestig calls it 'monumental' architecture, adding, 'People like monumentality, and I like to do things that look monumental. I like to see monumental things as well.' It may seem impossible to reconcile monumental with trendy, but the success of the Culture Club's design lies in its ability to do just that.

Guests can peer down on the Large Room crowd from behind dark glass panels that line the hallway between the Large Room and the smaller room on the first floor.

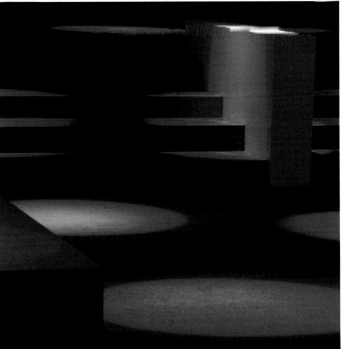

Top right: By staggering the heights of the overhead canopies and varying the lighting programmes in each, Sestig developed different lighting atmospheres within each sub-area of the Large Room. Above right: Lighting strips integrated into gaps between ceiling and wall panels emphasize the raw planes of the space.

In creating a subtly detailed club interior, Ivan Missinne for E&L Projects draws inspiration for **Kant** from the finest lace of Bruges.

Once home to a citadel protecting against Norman invaders and currently a UNESCO heritage site, the charming medieval town of Bruges has showcased the finest of Belgian lace for centuries. In dozens of shops throughout the provincial capital of West Flanders, lace rivals Belgian chocolate as a flourishing Flemish tourist attraction. But there's a new kind of lace in town. The visitor who mentions 'kant' (the Dutch word for 'lace') in Bruges nowadays may find himself directed to a restaurant/lounge fusion created by Ivan Missinne for E&L Projects and launched by Filip Tijssens – a venue without a doily or frill in sight. Although the unusual name does have its roots in the

concept of lace, it is based on the creative team's initial discussions, which broached the subject of shaping the visitor's experience. As Missinne explains, they wanted to do something that would involve what he calls 'both a micro and a macro scale'. They envisioned a patron entering the space, getting an overall impression and discovering the details only after being there for a while. 'Lace perfectly captures this notion,' says Missinne. 'If you see it from a distance, it's a white cloth. It's only up close that you see the finesse and beauty that's found in a piece of lace.'

The entrance to Kant, rendered in gold, offers card-carrying members the

Previous page: With their attention drawn to the striking portraits behind the bar, guests may fail to notice the lack of lamps above the bar. 'Normally the first thing designers do is hang fittings,' says designer Ivan Missinne, who opted to use light emanating from the photographs to illuminate the area, making the bar itself less of a focal point.

choice between a black curtain to the left, which leads to the restaurant, and a white curtain to the right, which conceals the bar and lounge area. The choice of left or right, and of black or white, falls into the category of Missinne's 'macro elements'. Sweeping the white curtain aside, the visitor is greeted by several more elements in the same category. At the far end of the room, a large globular light – the No Fruit lamp by Dark – hangs from a circular cutout made in the dropped ceiling above a circular platform. A series of photographic portraits set against a background of fluorescent light lines the wall to the right. Missinne commissioned photographer Ronald Stoops and make-up artist Inge Grognard to create these portraits. 'The photography gives a human touch to the architecture,' says Missinne. 'It was a big risk to work with pictures that have such a strong presence. They really had to be the right ones.' A final 'macro' touch are the walls composed of green Plexiglas rectangles clad in silver, which divide the main space from a smaller, more intimate front room. Another photograph, a picture of two children, presides here. 'In the main space, the music is quite loud,' explains Missinne. 'The front room, with its big lounge chair, invites a more private tête-à-tête. You can almost lie down here – really get comfortable. And the picture of the children

'Kant' is Dutch for 'lace'; Missinne wanted patrons to experience the bar as they might experience lace, first noticing the overall texture and then settling in on the intricate details, like arresting seating objects and cutouts in the lowered ceiling. Changing colours alter the mood of the interior.

As in a conversation or a song, it is the small, striking features of an interior that stand out and become what people remember best.

Watching over the intimate front room, which is set off by a dividing wall of green Plexiglas rectangles mounted in a silver frame, is a portrait of children, the work of photographer Ronald Stoops and make-up artist Inge Grognard. 'The photography gives a human touch to the architecture,' says Missinne. 'It was a big risk to work with pictures that have such a strong presence.'

'It was a big risk to work with pictures that have such a strong presence. They really had to be the right ones.' Ivan Missinne

gives mothers something to talk about.'

Once visitors have ensconced themselves in the club, the smaller, subtler details begin to reveal themselves. Little mirror balls rotate within several holes cut into the ceiling. A reflective black wall quietly picks up the shifting colours of the lights. Most of the lighting is generated by fluorescent lamps behind the photographs, which are dual printed, front and back, on polyester screens. 'Normally, the first thing designers do is hang fittings,' says Missinne. 'But we used the pictures to light up the bar. We needed the bar, but we didn't want to make it the centre point.'

The darker furnishings blend into the background, but thanks to engaging details, they are perfectly capable of withstanding close scrutiny. Contrasting with the mouldings and details of the shell of the building, which the designers were obliged to leave intact, are Philippe Starck's smoothly contoured Tooth stool, Tokujin Yoshioka's Tokyo Pop stool and Prospero Rasulo's Twist chair. The undulating curves of Verner Panton's Phantom seat and the unexpected cutouts in custom-designed, stainless-steel tables reward contemplation. Although Missinne considers himself an architect, his total involvement with each project extends to include the tiniest element. 'I'm proud of making the

concept and of taking it all the way through discussions with the electricians –
even to the point of deciding on ashtrays and on what kinds of shakers for salt
and pepper,' says Missinne, who believes it is details that people remember.
'We didn't want too much of the budget to be spent on expensive materials.
We wanted the money to go into the pictures – and not into floors or ceilings.'
As in a conversation or a song, it is the small, striking features of an interior
that stand out and become what people remember best.

Darker furnishings along the side wall seem to recede from view. Black mirrors used together with custom bench seating, stainless-steel tables and Verner Panton's Phantom chairs contribute to a composition interesting enough to reward closer scrutiny.

A former Barcelona warehouse inspires Antoni Arola and Minos Digenis to turn up the heat: the result is **Oven**, a multifunctional home-away-from-home.

From laid-back, Sunday-afternoon sushi parties to exhibition openings, concerts and dancing, partners Minos Digenis and DJ Angel Dust imagined that Oven, the restaurant/bar/lounge/club they envisioned for their converted printing-factory space in Barcelona's industrial Poblenou area, would do it all. Architect Digenis, always on the lookout for collaborative talent, approached Antoni Arola, famous for lighting, furnishing and perfume packaging designs, as well as interior work in other succesful project across Spain, to assist in developing the project. The two discovered wide overlap in their ideas about the way the space should feel.

As a metaphor for an interior centred on eating and entertainment, functionally flexible and suitable for round-the-clock use, the concept of the home was a perfect candidate. 'The main functions we outlined were listening to music and eating,' says Arola. 'In a home there are two poles: the kitchen, which is related to food, and the living and dining rooms, which are related to activities such as sitting, dining, listening to music, enjoying audio-visuals and taking life easy.' With these two poles in mind, Arola and Digenis drafted plans that would encourage visitors to approach the space as they would their homes. Digenis's conversion removed the first 12 metres of roof from the building, creating

Previous page: Designer Antoni Arola compares the glass wall that sets off the kitchen and allows curious diners to view activities within to the window of an oven. A suspended lampshade designed by graphic artist Pablo Martín features photos of gas-cooker flames, while kitchen utensils dangle below. Above: In converting the factory into a club, designers Antoni Arola and Minos Digenis preserved several existing elements, including this breeze-block wall.

'As its name indicates, the Lounge represents the room in a home where one tends to relax sitting down.'

Antoni Arola

Martin came up with the candle concept that spells out the club's name. This page, above: When not decked with tables, a small stage at the rear of the dining area is used for performances and dancing, underlining Oven's desire to be a multipurpose venue.

an enclosed garden. Passing through the garden, a feature of many Spanish residences, guests arrive in the Lounge. 'As its name indicates,' says Arola, 'the Lounge represents the room in a home where one tends to relax sitting down.' A serene haven for cultural activities, the Lounge has a lowered ceiling, for even more intimacy, and a predominance of red, which wraps it in a warm glow. A large, colour-changing lamp overhead serves as a defining element. Struggling to find the right lighting solution for the space, one of the team's designers added a small coloured globe light to the maquette; the team liked the effect so much that they built it to scale. Manufacturers Santa & Cole currently

market the final design of the luminaire, fittingly enough, as the Oven lamp. Next up in the linear sequence of spaces, still following the domestic example, is the dining area. Arrangements of custom-built tables and chairs, paired with less formal bench seating, carry over the easy feeling of the Lounge. When not covered with dining tables, part of the seating area is elevated to provide a stage and dance floor. Also integrated into the dining area are an intricate fibre-optic lighting object and a distorted mirror behind the bar. Diners are privy to a flurry of kitchen activity visible through a glass wall. Arola compares the framed wall, and the view of what is cooking in the

The designers blended the domestic metaphor and the accompanying cosy atmosphere with simple, often raw, industrial materials, many of which were taken from the original warehouse.

kitchen, to the window of an oven. He says that 'a large cylindrical suspended lamp whose shade is printed with photos of gas-cooker flames was an original idea of our graphic artist, Pablo Martín. The lamp floats over the main working surface with kitchen utensils hanging under it, a very distinguishable visual feature which adds a touch of personality to this area.' Martín was also behind the arrangement of candles that spells out the name 'Oven' in the breeze-block wall running the length of the space.

Part of the original factory, the wall is one of several industrial leftovers that offset the homy atmosphere. Concrete floors were left in place and waxed, the joints filled with resin. The slanted roof of the original building was also left intact, accentuated by a set of tilting screens overhead that receive projected images, while simultaneously acting as both acoustic elements and reflectors for Arola and Digenis's intricate lighting solution. The industrial feel is picked up in a number of simply finished raw materials, such as pine bar counters and tabletops made of folded iron sheeting. The lack of polish reflects a characteristic found in much of the designer's work. Like the intentional mistakes in Arabian carpets, the slight imperfections and plain surfaces in Arola's spaces feel inherently human, down to earth and part of a world that anyone can relate to.

In converting the factory, Digenis removed the first 12 metres of roof from the building, creating an enclosed garden, a feature common to many Spanish residences.

Oven does its utmost to make visitors feel at home. 'The main functions we outlined were listening to music and eating,' says Arola. 'In a home there are two poles: the kitchen, which is related to food, and the living and dining rooms, which are related to activities such as sitting, dining, listening to music, enjoying audio-visuals and taking life easy.'

Combining filmic elements with classic materials and Plexiglas, Ora-Ïto draws on a past in product design to create a futuristic interior for Parisian club **Cab.**

One might say that Ora-Ïto, the young French designer behind the hot Parisian team bearing his name, was the first Information-Age designer. As an intrepid 21-year-old with little more than a Mac and a corporate photocopy budget, he spurred an internet phenomenon with his sleek renderings of theoretical products for well-known brands: the Apple Hack-Mac, a camouflage laptop for the urban warrior; the Bic Atomic, the world's first lighter fuelled by nuclear energy; and the Gucci mansion, a designer residence fully stocked and ready for occupancy. Notoriety quickly became fame as the brands targeted by Ora-Ïto's goading designs began to commission actual products from the young talent.

The designer sees his early work less as teasing and more as looking beyond current time frames: 'My trick was to see further than the brands were seeing. Although I work for some of those brands today, my attitude remains the same.' He says that his ideas have always demonstrated a futuristic outlook. As a youngster aiming at big names, however, he 'just did it without asking permission'. While he may have broadened his scope beyond product design, if the interior for Cab is any evidence, Ora-Ïto's vision is still firmly fixed on the future. Client Philippe Fatien selected Ora-Ïto to create a new club and bar, an extension to their successful Cabaret restaurant, in large part because of the

Previous page: Ora-Ïto's background in product design translates into sculptural, watertight forms. Many, like the bar pictured, have integrated LED lighting. Above: LEDs are hidden behind Plexiglas corner panels; bench seating is comprised of padded leather strips.

commotion surrounding the designer. 'They wanted press coverage and an image,' he says. 'They wanted more than just a designer with a nice style.' It was his reputation as 'a phenomenon' that sealed his selection. Ora-Ïto was given an aesthetic wild card to implement the design as he saw fit. Fatien's gamble paid off in an elegant yet cutting-edge interior that has made Cab an unqualified success in the flighty Parisian night scene. 'We wanted to make a club that was a cross between James Bond and *Tron*, something very wild and futuristic,' is Ora-Ïto's succinct description of the final design. He mentions the use of 'classic materials like leather, all teak wood, lots of colour and Plexiglas' and stresses

the desire to make guests feel as though they are 'not on earth but in a spaceship'. It's no coincidence that Ora-Ïto's reference points aren't interiors per se. His rich language of design features forms and gadgets reflects his roots in the world of products. It's a vocabulary that extends to Cab as a whole. In the words of the designer, 'The club really looks like an object – like an object in a big box.' The box Ora-Ïto refers to is both the shell of the building and a wooden ribbon that glides along the ceilings, orientating club-goers and housing the lighting in cutaway sections, while wrapping around to partially enclose areas of the interior such as the DJ booth and the remarkable seating arrangement in the

Mirrored walls backing the alcoves visually double the depth of these recessed areas, thus eliminating any sense of spatial restriction.

Ora-Ïto's rich language of design features forms and gadgets that reflect his roots in the world of products.

Top: In the Salle Doughnut, circular leather 'doughnuts' embracing Corian tables rise from a stage, turning a seating area into an alien landscape. Above: The doughnut hole and leather panelling motifs are combined in another set of alcoves. 'As in a car, there is leather everywhere,' says Ora-Ïto.

so-called Salle Donut. Here the edge of a raised Corian stage, with a panel of glass connecting to it, curves towards the ceiling. Rising from the stage are four circular leather couches; the 'doughnut holes' at the centre of these sofas accommodate tables also made of Corian. A similar motif is echoed in surrounding alcoves, where parallel strips of leather panelling line all four sides, with holes providing the necessary space for patrons' legs. 'As in a car, there is leather everywhere,' says Ora-Ïto, who worked with Swiss manufacturer De Sedeto create the custom seating. In collaboration with specialists, Ora-Ïto crafted a complicated lighting system that bathes the interior in patterns of colour that can shift from electric, saturated shades to a softer, more calming scheme. Together with a range of surfaces adapted to projections used for gatherings like company parties, the variability of the lighting makes the club a highly flexible space for festive events. Making Cab attractive enough to host parties for diverse organizations, while building up an intriguing identity for the space itself, required a delicate touch. But Ora-Ïto is no stranger to the complex workings of image, which he's been studying since his early days as a renegade designer. Referring to his early projects, he says that he pictured himself as the art director of the various brands, someone in a position to 'understand their desire, their history, their identity'.

The edge of the Salle Doughnut stage curves upwards to support a glass partition that serves as a screen for projected images.

'We wanted to make a club that was a cross between James Bond and *Tron*, something very wild and futuristic,' explains the designer.

Cinnamon Club Bar.

Introducing a large projection wall and backlit curtains, Mueller Kneer Associates make a tight, windowless basement bar in London luminous and airy.

As MPs, politicians and other luminaries dine upstairs at the ultra-refined Cinnamon Club, one of London's top-flight Indian restaurants, members of a hipper generation imbibe cocktails in the *haute glamour* of the bar downstairs. The Cinnamon Club Bar is riding the crest of a wave of new private bars washing over the famed nightlife of London. These seem to be emerging from the same spirit of free-market privatization that has seized Tony Blair's New Labour government; in this case, it is solving one of British nightlife's thornier problems: the draconian liquor licensing which impels pubs and bars to shut their doors often before midnights on weekends. With entrepreneurs having struggled for years to get around this dilemma, watering holes such as Milk & Honey, Abigail's Party, Floral House and, now, the Cinnamon Club Bar have finally hit upon the solution: go private. Assuming members-only status allows them not only to operate until much later, but also to provide intimate atmospheres for their select patrons. 'They're like urban living rooms,' says Olaf Kneer of design team Mueller Kneer Associates, responsible for the creation of the Cinnamon Club Bar. 'It's quite an exciting thing, and a real counterpoint to the standard high-street pubs.'

Previous page: Mueller Kneer delicately masked the close confines of the space, using backlit curtains against the walls. Above: A large video wall takes up one side of the room, creating 'living wallpaper' from seamlessly synchronized video images.

Not that the Cinnamon Club Bar was ever in danger of seeming generic. The bar is the latest addition to a 1,115-square-metre 'gastronomic enterprise'; the sprawling Cinnamon Club consists of several dining venues (restaurant, breakfast room, private members' area) ensconced in the converted Old Westminster Library. While the Club plays host to the upper crust, the brief to designers bidding on the bar project was to devise a transitional, contrasting space to attract a more nightlife-savvy crowd. According to Marianne Mueller, 'The bar was the little gem of the development. They wanted the downstairs to be contemporary European in feeling,

and a bit of an antidote to the space upstairs. How we tackled it was to look at the larger context. We wanted an element of surprise.' In this case, the designers were faced with an approach that leads downstairs, through several dark and more classical rooms, to the bar itself, housed in a closed-off, undramatic space. The team's proposal attempted to counterbalance these drawbacks, says Mueller, adding that the result 'feels incredibly luminous and airy'. 'We wanted to expand the boundaries of the space, to remove a sense of perimeters, so we used backlit curtains against the walls. It's light and almost windswept, quite an incredible experience for a space that is cut off from

'We wanted to expand the boundaries of the space, so we used backlit curtains against the walls.'

Marianne Mueller

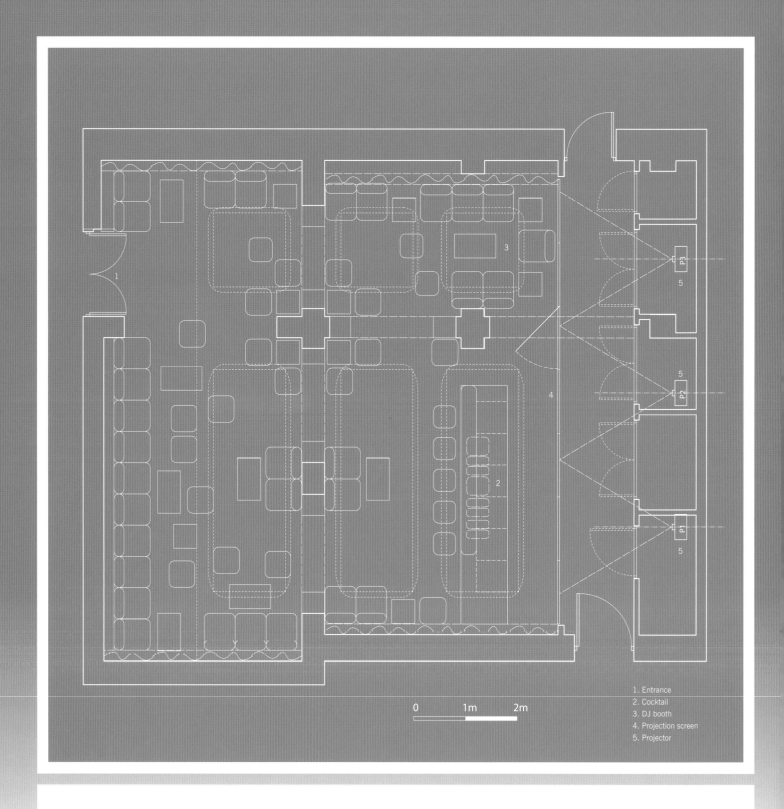

1. Entrance
2. Cocktail
3. DJ booth
4. Projection screen
5. Projector

0   1m   2m

the elements.' Mueller Kneer introduced a massive 9-metre-wide, 2.5-metre-high projection surface, which makes up one entire wall and acts as a sort of artificial window. Projectors mounted in a narrow corridor behind the wall have been carefully synchronized to create a seamless 'living wallpaper' along the length of the expanse, a dynamic canvas for various graphics, installations and even a live satellite broadcast on opening night featuring Talvin Singh, India's premier DJ, performing live from Bombay.

Though the space is compact, it never feels tight, in part because Mueller Kneer rejected the owner's original request for a higher seating capacity in favour of a solution providing more variety. 'The space is very small, but there are different microenvironments. It's bright by the bar; the girls sitting by the bar have these beautiful silhouettes. Back on the sofas, it's darker and cosier. Intimacy was very important.' Arches and imported tables make the place vaguely Indian, but Mueller Kneer were hesitant to make unduly direct references. 'We didn't necessarily take the look from an Indian typology,' says Mueller. 'Instead, we looked at a subject – in this case, Hindu temples and Art Nouveau – along with the idea of luminosity, and constructed it from there.'

Lining the illuminated bar, which is open and bright, are seemingly weightless Knoll bar stools. 'Back on the sofas, it's darker and cosier,' says Marianne Mueller, who adds that 'intimacy was very important'.

Where other designers might simply see these as styles to reproduce, Mueller Kneer find them to be more fertile grounds. 'References are very important for us, and we take great care to finely balance them. What is important for us in our designs is, on the one hand, the construction of situations, or events, and on the other hand, stories and narratives, or history.'

Cinnamon Club is one of a new breed of members-only bars in London that offer a more intimate social setting for a select coterie. 'They're like urban living rooms,' says Olaf Kneer.

Claiming 'change' as his motto, David Collins reinvented **Kabaret's Prophecy**, now a real-time, ever-evolving club in London's Soho area.

With a deft touch at expressing luxury, designer David Collins has long been the go-to guy for posh retail and hotel projects in the UK, as illustrated by a clientele that includes Vivienne Westwood, Jaeger, Victoria's Secret and London's famed restaurateur Marco Pierre White. But his latest project, Kabaret's Prophecy, amply demonstrates that Collins' instincts are no less sharp when aiming at hip rather than just high-end. This is due as much to the designer's astute choice of partners as it is to his own creative talent. 'We like to collaborate,' Collins explains. 'You get a better result. More and more, I've begun collaborating with other people to achieve different looks.' Collins

began with the notion of a space marrying opulent finishes with cutting-edge technology. Inspired by the dynamic walls of D-Edge in São Paolo (see pages 246-253), Collins imagined a perpetually-changing backdrop for Kabaret's Prophecy: 'I wanted everything to be able to move, ranging from William Morris wallpapers to cityscapes at night, and I didn't want it to look like a video box.' One result of his concept is the club's captivating central feature: the undulating and hypnotically dynamic digital wallpaper. David Collins enlisted the skills of United Visual Artists – pioneering environmental-graphics engineers and live-performance-video specialists – to develop the unique, moving LED architecture.

Previous page: A central feature of the space, the pewter bar is inlaid with Swarovski crystals illuminated by ultraviolet LEDs. The crystals trace a rococo pattern, also applied to the punched leather of the seating. Top left: Collins enlisted the help of crystal manufacturer Swarovski to transform an antique chandelier into this striking piece near the entrance. Top right: Although the Verner Panton lamps are relatively large, their transparency made them

'People love fiddling around with it and doing new programs, everything from hippy trippy flowers to more architectural graphics.' David Collins

unimposing enough to meet the designer's requirements. Opposite page, bottom and above: The club's spectacular digital wallpaper can display anything from 3-D logos and graphics to full video content. Nearly 3000 4-by-4-cm Barco MiPIX units make up a canvas. Images can be manipulated by means of a real-time generator or 'mixed' to the beat of music in real-time with a MIDI keyboard, resulting in an ever-changing environment.

Comprised of units of Barco's MiPIX system, the wall installation is capable of displaying everything from three-dimensional logos and graphics to full video content. Nearly 3000 4-x-4-centimetre units make up the two canvases that wrap smoothly around the contours of the room and into its alcoves. In total, the installation measures over 17 metres long and 1 metre high. The state-of-the-art-system allows images to be created via a real-time generator or 'mixed' with a MIDI keyboard, which makes for an ever-changing tableau of moods. The graphic possibilities are endless. 'People love fiddling around with it and doing new programs, everything from hippy-trippy flowers to more architectural graphics,' says Collins. For the wall adornments in the bathroom, Collins approached another artist, Jamie Hewlett, the famed illustrator behind the *Tank Girl* and *Gorillaz* characters. 'I thought it would be cool, instead of having the toilets "graffiti'd", to put graffiti in the toilets myself,' says Collins. Hewlett created a cast of scuffed and sultry characters to occupy the bathroom walls. In the otherwise slick-as-silicone space, characterized by cool dark colours highly suggestive of electronics or computers, Hewlett's drawings add a precious note of human-faced irreverence. For all the collaboration that went into developing Kabaret's Prophecy, Collins' own contributions do not miss their mark.

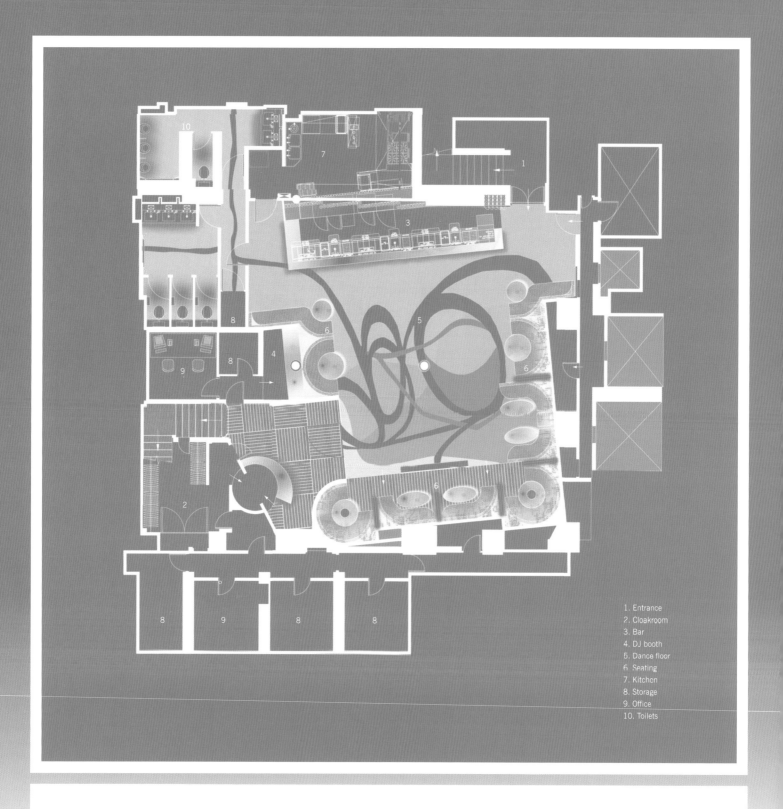

1. Entrance
2. Cloakroom
3. Bar
4. DJ booth
5. Dance floor
6. Seating
7. Kitchen
8. Storage
9. Office
10. Toilets

'We wanted it to be comfortable in terms of materials, including the punched-leather and curved asymmetrical banquettes,' he says. Lavish custom touches, which Collins has described as 'maximalism', drive home the look. 'The bar is designed as a big feature,' notes Collins. 'It's pewter inlaid with Swarovski crystal, illuminated with ultraviolet LED.' Crystals in the bar are arranged in a pattern mimicking that of the punched leather of the seating. Equally rococo is the antique chandelier at the entrance, a custom-refurbished, black laser-lit piece hung with jet crystals by Swarovski. To emphasize the moods created by the walls, Collins used reflective surfaces (pewter bar front, crystals, mirrors) and a monochromatic palette of warm greys for the walls and the laser-cut floor covering. Thanks to the different tones and finishes, light bounces back in different intensities, adding depth to the space. An overhead canopy of laser-lighting provides extra illumination. Also designed by Levine, the canopy adds to the dancing play of reflections picked up by the surfaces in Kabaret's Prophecy. The club's unusual name comes from its previous life here in London's Soho area, where it was formerly known as Murray's Cabaret. Collins explains the turnover as a consequence of the limited number of licences available in London. But he also believes that the fickle nature of nightlife demands frequent change.

Kabaret's Prophecy features state-of-the-art sound and audio systems in addition to the advanced lighting technology.

One result of Collins' concept is the club's captivating central feature: the undulating and hypnotically dynamic digital wallpaper.

Top and above left: 'I thought it would be cool, instead of having the toilets "graffiti'd", to put graffiti there myself,' says Collins. Enter Jamie Hewlett, the famed illustrator behind the *Tank Girl* and *Gorillaz* characters, who conjured up a cast of sexy, brooding players for rest-room walls.

'Clubs have to constantly be reinventing themselves,' says Collins. In designing Kabaret's Prophecy, with its infinitely mutable backdrop and furnishings that reflect its colours and moods, Collins and his collaborators have created the ultimate: a club that can reinvent itself in real-time, at the touch of a button.

Rendered in a monochromatic palette of warm greys, the laser-cut floor covering picks up the coloured lighting to varying degrees, adding depth to the space.

At **Le Carrousel** in Nantes, Hazard Studio dazzles guests with a soufflé of colours, materials and styles in a Jules Verne-inspired atmosphere of 'smooth chaos'.

Looking at the interior design of Le Carrousel in Nantes, France, one would be forgiven for not immediately recalling the stories of Jules Verne, most of which feature interiors only in the form of whizz-bang contraptions – time machines, hot-air balloons, submarines and the like – lined with whirling dials and pumping pistons. But the writer, a native of Nantes, was in fact the starting point chosen by Hazard Studio and its clients in developing plans for Le Carrousel. 'We started the project talking about Jules Verne,' says Alfredo Rodriguez, owner and director of Hazard Studio. 'We wanted a voyage through experiences and sensations. We decided to express those feelings through colours, materials and different styles.'

Le Carrousel is anything but retro. And despite its ties to Verne, in an aesthetic sense it steers well clear of the Nantes vernacular. 'Nantes is quite traditional, and normally the people are very quiet and don't like big changes,' says Rodriguez, whose initial aim was to 'present this club differently'. In other words, Le Carrousel was slated from the start to attract the chic and fashion-conscious to a space befitting them. At the same time, Hazard was not afraid to serve up a contemporary recipe laced with a healthy dose of classicism. Rodriguez 'wanted to show history', while also creating an interior that would look 'old and modern at the same time'. To get to what Rodriguez calls 'another space in history', visitors pass through a striking entrance tunnel lined

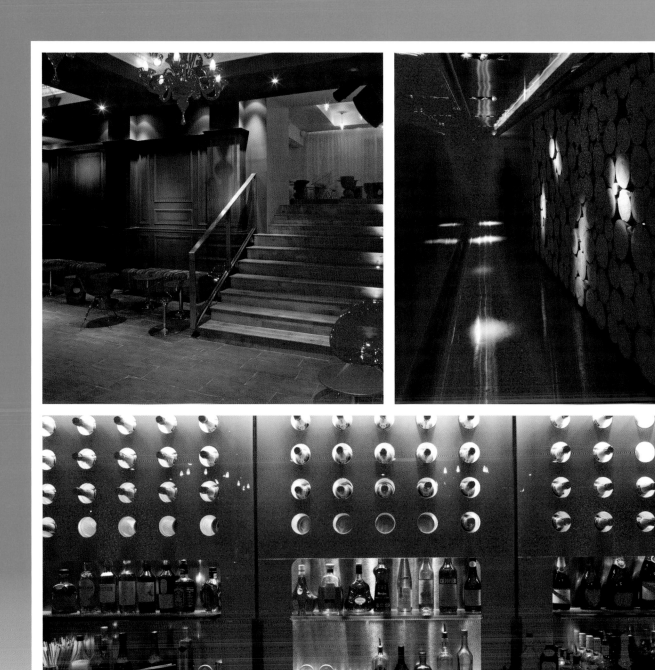

Top left: In the Main Room, moulded ceilings and walls, as well as chandeliers, imbue the space with a classical feel. Top right: The entrance tunnel is lined floor to ceiling with brushed stainless steel; one wall is comprised entirely of stacked, untreated tree trunks. Their sawed-off ends form an abstract geometric pattern repeated by mirrors in the Main Room. Above: Radiantly illuminated in red, the Main Room has also been called the Red Room.

floor to ceiling with brushed stainless steel, one wall of which is made up entirely of stacked, untreated tree trunks, whose evenly coloured, sawed-off ends become an abstract geometric pattern along the wall. 'When drawing this tunnel, we tried to create a psychological distance between the outside and the inside, to stretch out the desire to get to the bar,' explains the designer. Narrowed significantly by the presence of the logs, the tunnel is an effective contrast to the size of the Main Room, making the latter seem larger upon arrival. In the Main Room, ceiling mouldings and chandeliers give the project what Rodriguez describes as a 'classical breath'. Nonetheless, chandeliers made of red Lucite and, along one side, an illuminated red

bar-front do away with any possible fussiness. Cool slate floors complete the look and offset the playful plastics, while complementing the more traditional elements. Rodriguez refers to the overall image as 'smooth chaos' and offers the repetition of circular forms as an example, adding that even though guests may enjoy varying experiences in this space, he and his team have injected a sense of continuity, through repetitive details, that creates a coherently comfortable context. He draws a connection between the round tree trunks in the entrance tunnel and the circular mirrors clustered behind the DJ area. 'Chaos is when you have no reference to anything, but let your mind go,' he says. 'The tree trunks and the mirrors are different,

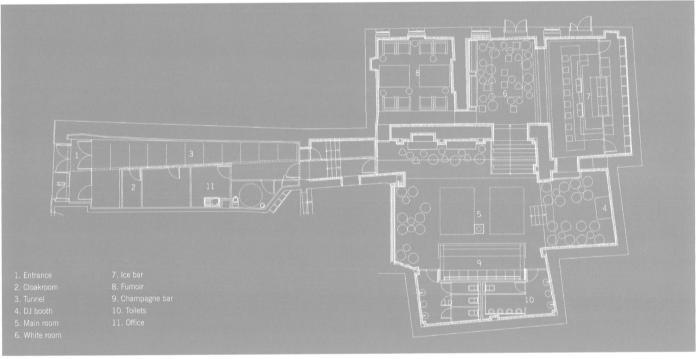

1. Entrance
2. Cloakroom
3. Tunnel
4. DJ booth
5. Main room
6. White room
7. Ice bar
8. Fumoir
9. Champagne bar
10. Toilets
11. Office

Top left: The Ice Bar, rendered entirely in white is 'a pure space' in the eyes of Rodriguez. With a view to the Main Room, those in the Ice Bar never feel cut off. Top right: Explaining how the design team envisioned the visitor's journey through the club, Rodriguez says: 'Chaos is when you have no reference to anything, but let your mind go. Repetition takes people from one place to another smoothly, giving an impression of déjà vu.'

but the shape is the same. Repetition takes people from one place to another smoothly, giving an impression of déjà vu.' Guests walk out of the Main Room and into the White Room, which in turn lends access to their final destination, the Ice Bar. In the White Room, the dominant colour shifts abruptly from red to white, but Hazard transitions other changes more gradually, repeating much of the furniture from the Main Room in white and clear colours. Walls are treated with white curtains and iridescent white and mother-of-pearl mosaics. As opposed to the feverish Main Room, the mood here is 'pure and relaxing', says Rodriguez. 'Relaxing' is a good term for the overall ambience at Le Carrousel, which is, in fact, not really a club at all, but – as it

bills itself – a 'music bar'. Rodriguez explains this genre-mixing as a product of necessity rather than as a purely innovative move on the part of the designers. He says that, in terms of official rules and regulations, a club is defined as playing music 'at or under 105 decibels'. 'Here, we have neighbours living upstairs, so we can't go over 95 decibels'. 'Another apt definition of the general mood here is 'active lounging', backed by DJs providing a discerning mix of music. 'It's a meeting place where people can talk to each other,' says Rodriguez. 'The music is important, just to create the right atmosphere.' A complicated balance of elements, yes, but Le Carrousel enfolds its clientele in the perfect state of equilibrium.

At **Rehab**, a 17th-century warehouse in Leeds now attracting the post-chemical club generation, Igloo Design scatters references to the medical world.

Since 1991, the award-winning Leeds club Back to Basics has been attracting world-class DJs and discerning clubbers from all over the UK with a simple formula: great music plus great attitude equals success. But a decade in club years is a long time. The scene evolves, and the loyal base of followers grows up too, to be replaced with younger and younger crops of new clubbers. For his new club project, Rehab, Dave Beer, one of Basics' founders, wanted to appeal to that loyal, but maturing, base. Like Beer, Back to Basics' clientele had grown older and possibly wiser, and their tastes had ripened with them. According to Soo Wilkinson, one of the partners behind Igloo Design, the firm that Beer tapped to create the interior for Rehab, 'Dave was feeling like it was

time to do something a bit more sophisticated, with the kind of design normally reserved for hotels and restaurants.' While keeping with the unencumbered spirit of Back to Basics, Igloo and Beer aimed at a middle ground between super-clubs, such as Cream and Ministry, and a new breed of nightlife establishment, the DJ bar, a smaller 'boutique' space for music aficionados. 'We were trying to make something that was quite new in nightclub culture in the UK, while staying true to house-music roots,' says Wilkinson. 'Our ethos was to create a space with a synergy of all the elements - sound, lighting, aesthetics and ambience were treated with equal importance,'

Previous page: Set in a 17th-century warehouse and catering to a discerning crowd of clubbers, Rehab boasts an interior that mixes fine original detailing with massive, sculptural furniture and modern finishes. Above: Clubbers on the mezzanine-level dance floor, which features its own DJs and sound system, can peer down on the main floor through a soundproof glass divider.

The bold colours of the bar area and the furniture grab visitors' attention, leaving the darker, unadorned dance-floor area to recede into the background.

Wilkinson and her clients altered the average house club's ratio of dance-floor space to seating space to favour lounging and drinking. Bulky, geometric furniture from the likes of Ron Arad and Liverpool-based Definitive contrasts with the more delicate mouldings and plasterwork.

Having secured a space for the club, a building that started life as a 17th-century warehouse, the team focused on the right balance of functions for this new type of environment. Igloo and its clients altered the average house club's ratio of dance-floor space to seating space to favour lounging and drinking. 'This is, after all, a nightclub for Back to Basics, so the dance floor is a major part of the experience,' says the designer. 'It's a dark area, a fixed and smoky place where you can lose yourself completely in the music. The lighting was key here, along with the biggest mirror ball we could find. For Rehab, the main design area was the lounge. It used to be that people didn't really go to clubs to talk to each other,' she adds, referring to a practice that Rehab has sought to change.

The bold colours of the bar area and the furniture grab visitors' attention, leaving the darker, unadorned dance-floor area to recede into the background. Not permitted to alter the original features of the building, Igloo clad the walls in ebony veneer, fabric and mirrors. The furniture, mostly white and red, stands out against the darker background. Igloo selected massive and geometric forms created by the likes of Ron Arad and the Liverpool-based company Definitive to offset the more delicate details found in mouldings and plasterwork.
For a touch of glamour, the team installed a 3-metre-high Venetian chandelier, which shimmers opulently over the lounge area. The seating arrangement provides guests with a complete overview of the space. Wilkinson remarks that

Dave Beer, owner of Rehab and the man behind the legendary UK club Back to Basics, knew that to attract the more mature clubber, music would have to be top-notch. Rehab's niche is somewhere between the super-club (Cream, Ministry) and the 'boutique' DJ bar: intimate, but with a world-class sound system for A-list DJs.

no matter where you sit, 'you can see everywhere else. It makes for a collective experience.' The mezzanine-level dance floor, which features its own DJs and sound system, is cut off from the main space by glazed partitions that allow patrons in both areas to exchange glances. 'Upstairs has a completely different vibe,' says Wilkinson, 'so it looks like people are dancing out of tune.' Peppering the space are nods to medicine, from the red and white of the furniture to smaller details. 'The name Rehab injects a sense of humour into the space. Dave joked that we were providing for the "post-chemical" generation of clubbers - his brief was to create a mixture of Harley Street Clinic and Studio 54 - so we included lots of cheeky medical references. The upstairs day beds are shrinks' couches. We placed medical equipment behind the bars. And the staff are dressed in doctors' and nurses' uniforms, complete with stethoscopes to keep a check on the club's pulse.' Ashtrays in the lacquered-wood bar upstairs are surgical emesis basins. 'As you walk into the space, past the pay points and the cloakroom,' she says, 'you see a medical case containing specimen jars filled with red liquid.' The case also holds packets of pills labelled with such lofty promises as 'Learn to Play Guitar in an Instant', 'Clone Your Best Mate's Girlfriend' and 'Become a Virgin Again', created by the

Visually arresting, the bold colours of lights and furniture in the bar area put the focus on socializing. The darker, cooler dance floor, which is relatively plain in contrast, recedes into the background.

'Our ethos was to create a space with a synergy of all the elements – sound, lighting, aesthetics and ambience were treated with equal importance.'

Soo Wilkinson

Left: A large chandelier over the dance floor is Igloo's token nod to the classical heritage of the building. The rest mixes bold furniture with humorous references to medicine, such as psychiatrists' couches on the mezzanine and surgical emesis basins used as ashtrays. Right: Not permitted to alter the original features of the listed building, Wilkinson and her team installed façades of ebony veneer, fabric and mirrors on the walls.

Dutch art collective Jesus Has a Sister.

The sense of humour at Rehab is an intangible element aimed at a more wizened and mischievous older crowd. These are people, says Wilkinson, who 'will always be interested in the music' but who are also looking for 'a sense of occasion' and a night out that calls for a bit of dressing up. 'Who wants to spend their hard-earned cash in a dump?' is her rhetorical conclusion. With sophisticated jibes and polished edges, good music and equally good conversation, Rehab gives them exactly what they want.

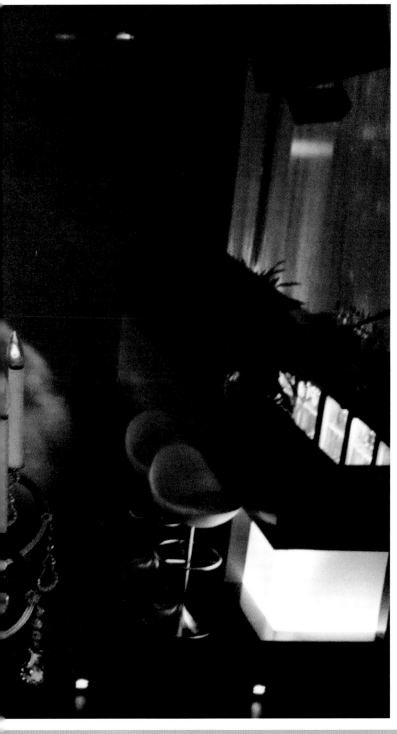

The interior of Manchester vodka bar **Babushka**, created by Lief Design, is sleekly modern, with a healthy dose of schlock thrown in for good measure.

Babushka is Russian for 'grandmother'; and indeed, the precious flocked wallpapers and roseate hues found inside the Manchester branch of Babushka, a successful chain of British vodka bars, appears to have crawled right out of the drawing room of a Chekhov dowager. But for the rest, Babushka's Manchester interior, created by Nottingham-based Lief Design, is sleek and modern, with a healthy dose of schlock thrown in for good measure. Having already established a handful of popular London locations, Babushka's owners, the successful conglomerate Style in the City, were ready to push out of the capital city into not only Nottingham and Manchester, but Bristol and

Glasgow as well. The eclectic second-hand interiors that had charmed locals in the London locations were not equipped to handle a multi-city expansion, however, nor would they survive the transition from small franchise to national brand. It was the task of Lief Design to bring the Babushka formula first to Nottingham, then Manchester, in such a way that it could become a template for future locations. Martin Vicker, principal designer for Lief, refers to the new look as 'theatrical, sleazy, and dark', explaining that it arose from a careful study of Babushka's other locations, as well as from ideas proposed by the owners. 'They aspired to something rich and flamboyant,' he says. 'They are

Previous page: Babushka's striped ceiling serves as both decoration and navigation. 'It allows you to get your bearings back when you've had a bit too much to drink,' says principal designer Martin Vicker. Above: A large void surrounded by a mezzanine puts the whole club on display. 'We quickly worked out that it was a see-and-be-seen venue,' says Vicker.

life-grabbing, fast-living clients, and the same is true of their clientele.' Vicker calls the London bars 'post junk shop' – venues 'not composed in quite the same way as the new ones would be'. Boasting a late license allowing it to stay open until 4 a.m., the latest location, with a full dance floor and a focus on music and DJs, reflects the glamour-power of the famous Manchester scene.

Tucked into a converted Victorian factory, the Print Works, the location is both a help and a hindrance. On rainy days (that is to say, frequently), queuing guests can take shelter under cover. But Babushka's loud-and-proud presence is visible to those outside only in a very thin strip of façade, the rest concealed inside and buried underground. To get the Babushka feeling across in such a small space, Lief packed the two windows flanking the mirrored logo with oversized, kitsch flower arrangements backed by custom-coloured flock wallpaper, also used extensively within.

Lief carried this tableau effect throughout the interior. Vicker says they envisioned a film set – 'either a really seedy dive or a luxury liner' – and patrons in 'different states of mind'. 'Some are quite straight and focused; others have maybe had a bit too much champagne. We put in enough signals,

Top: A window display featuring the club's signature flocked wallpapers and oversized flower arrangements is a coy hint to queuing patrons of the interior awaiting them. Above: Different seating areas create 'social flexibility,' says Vicker. 'We always like to give the clientele as much choice as possible.'

'The owners aspired to something rich and flamboyant. They are life-grabbing, fast-living clients, and the same is true of their clientele.'

Martin Vicker

Left and top right: The mixture of luxurious and kitschy materials gives the space what the designer calls a 'theatrical, sleazy and dark' look. Above right: Clad in the same flocked wallpaper, the DJ booth juts over the dance floor. A beaded chain curtain, sourced from an American military manufacturer, cordons off a more private seating area below.

symbols and values to create inspiration in everyone.' A close attention to detail, combined with ultra-vibrant colours and a careful mix of furnishings, gives the space a slightly self-conscious, even surreal, ambience. Even when furnishings are obscured by hordes of partygoers, eye candy remains visible: particularly striking are pink and purple stripes on the mezzanine ceiling. According to Vicker, Lief used the whole ceiling as a decorative styling element to make 'a deliberate statement'. 'It allows you to see any point in the space and to get your bearings back when you've had a bit too much to drink.'

The range of seating environments in the relatively compact club can pose a problem for the tipsy or indecisive guest: purpose-designed choices are benches backed by the signature wallpaper near the entrance and stools accompanied by tables on a narrow strip of the mezzanine. Upstairs, in the open lounge and VIP area, the selection includes recognizable pieces from such big names as Cattelan Italia and Johanson, which share the space with retro items specially sourced for the project, such as Artifort chairs, Pantela lights and 'Poodle' rugs.

The focus on feel rather than function is what Vicker believes will ultimately

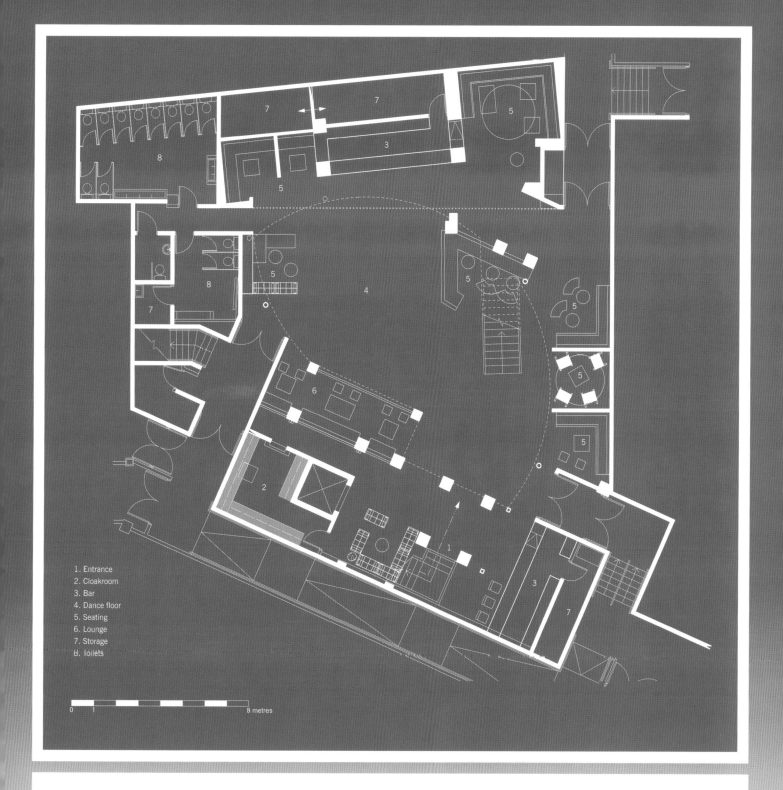

1. Entrance
2. Cloakroom
3. Bar
4. Dance floor
5. Seating
6. Lounge
7. Storage
8. Toilets

0   1   8 metres

determine the success or failure of the interior. In this respect, he compares

nightclubs to churches: 'Both are spiritual places, and neither has an involved

brief. In a church, you are dealing with seating and spiritual layout.

In a nightclub, there is the bar and the seating, and dancing and a DJ.

Unlike an office, there are not a lot of criteria. It's quite a special brief.'

Above: Lief installed white mosaic-covered columns to frame, and thus draw attention to, the second bar.

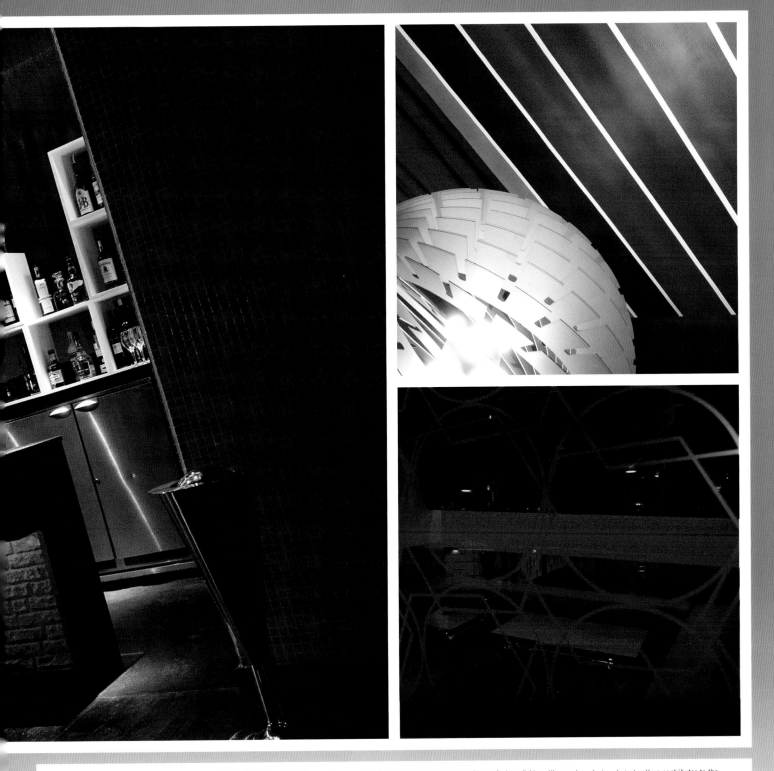

Top: A heavy curtain, striped wall and the Helios candelier by PS Interiors behind one of the bars adds to the burlesque atmosphere. Above: A glass divider with a custom-designed vinyl pattern contributes to the layering and mismatching of textures.

To watch and to be watched: Glasgow's **Collage Bar,** a project by Graven Images, gives the city a cosy new venue for people-watching.

When it comes to entrepreneurs with an interest in nightlife, many of them seem to think that bigger is better. But tucked away in a compact corner space in the Radisson SAS Hotel situated on Glasgow's bustling Argyle Street, the newly installed Collage Bar proves something that barflies have known all along, namely that cosier venues offer advantages of their own. In fact, the design team at Graven Images viewed the diminutive size as an asset rather than a liability. 'Some of Glasgow's best bars are small intimate spaces that don't rely on hordes of people to create an atmosphere,' says principal designer Jim Hamilton, 'and smaller bars are stronger all day long.' While Collage may not be able to

accommodate throngs of evening pub-crawlers with its 150-person capacity, it takes fewer patrons to build the critical mass for a lively atmosphere during the day. A stone's throw from Glasgow's Central Station, the bar is optimally positioned to take advantage of foot traffic and afternoon business appointments. Furthermore, even when Collage is not crammed to the hilt, the steady stream of faces going by ensures a sense of human connection. 'It's a people-watching bar,' says Hamilton. Graven Images emphasized this aspect by building the bar on two levels, strategically lowering the ground-floor slab by 400 millimetres to allow room in the low-ceilinged space for a mezzanine. The bi-level setup

Previous page: Indian silver greywood veneer trims the bar downstairs. Behind it, a large glass gantry reaching to the ceiling is stacked not with the customary liquor bottles, but rather – for a domestic touch – a collection of Scandinavian ceramics. Top: Back-painted green glass walls line a small nook under the mezzanine, drawing eyes to the depth of the space. Above left and right: Fixed booths and more open, raised seating provide private areas,

not only increases the overall floor space of the bar, but also optimizes views of Argyle Street through the glazed façade. Explains Hamilton, 'People sitting on the lowered ground floor are at a good height to people-watch without having to make eye contact with passers-by, while those on the upper level get a great view down to the street below.' The two levels also allow for a variation in ambience within the small space. 'The analogy we used is a double-decker bus,' he says. 'Downstairs you pay your money and ride, mingling with the crowd. On the upper level, the world is your oyster. You position yourself to watch and be watched.' 'One of the main design decisions was the shape of the mezzanine,' he continues.

'It was a fundamental space-saving move to follow the shape of the façade. From there, we took the decision early on to keep the material palette to a minimum.' Of course here, as in much of Graven Images' work, there is a depth of richness in the simplicity he implies, and it lies in the attention to detail, as illustrated in Hamilton's description of the process of choosing materials for the balustrading: 'Curved glass would have been too ostentatious, and we felt that using more hardwood could have been claustrophobic. We opted for edge-fixed glass fins set into milled steel frames, which add some privacy but are mostly transparent.' Curving canopies with book-matched veneers hover over the mezzanine tables,

as well as somewhat public spaces, within the bar. Above: Balustrades featuring perpendicularly mounted glass fins produce a rich, layered effect without overwhelming the small space.

creating private spaces, acoustically and visually, for patrons to conduct lunch meetings or more intimate chats. 'Within the canopies are the speaker system and lighting. A lot of things are contained within the lowered volumes, so as not to encroach on the glass façade,' says Hamilton. Graven Images economized on space by designing two-legged tables and back-to-back booth seats. The booths feature slots built into their ends to stow magazines and newspapers, big favourites of lone daytime patrons, as well as the lunch crowd. Both bar and walls are clad in Indian silver greywood veneer. The bar forms the central feature downstairs. Behind it, a large glass gantry that stretches to the ceiling is filled

not with the customary bottles of top-shelf liquors, but with ceramics. 'Most of them are Swedish, mixed with a few Danish pieces,' says Hamilton. 'They bring a bit of a domestic scale into the project. We were hoping to recreate the essence of a good house party in full swing.' While the design of a bar may be watertight, Hamilton believes other elements, such as service, food and music, are equally, if not more, important in luring patrons back time and again. And little touches – like a tasteful display of ceramics – help to differentiate one bar from all the others. 'Every bar should exude its own character,' he concludes, 'and whether you've been there once or a hundred times, it should always be welcoming.'

By putting the miracle of modern technology to work at **D-Edge**'s São Paulo branch, Muti Randolph reveals the secret structure of techno music.

At the climactic moment of *The Matrix*, the character Neo experiences a revelation in which the hidden code of the Matrix appears to him as flashing, cascading lines of green gibberish. Clubbers at D-Edge's São Paulo branch may experience a similar feeling as the underlying blips and beeps of the DJ's records are transformed into a pulsating, protean labyrinth of flashing bars of light. Here at D-Edge, the miracle of modern technology reveals the secret structure of techno music. The designer of D-Edge, Muti Randolph, makes no secret of his life-long fascination with computers, an obsession that launched the design of both the São Paulo location of D-Edge and the original, slightly older, club of the same name in Campo Grande. 'I didn't think about other clubs when creating the design,' he says. 'I thought about computers, electronic gadgets, audio equipment and computer graphics. The light grid in São Paulo is somewhat like a computer-generated wire frame.' In Campo Grande, the strong design features (notably the vivid colours and round plastic forms) team with painted walls depicting computer circuitry to create, in Randolph's words, 'a playful set of the interior of a computer'. Describing the newer interior, he emphasizes that 'in São Paulo, the computer is real'. Like a computer, D-Edge São Paulo is a black box housing extensive cables and

Previous page and above: At D-Edge, designer Muti Randolph set a grid of lighting strips into walls, floor and ceiling, and connected it to a central computer controlled by a light jockey (LJ). The LJ selects a range of lighting patterns from literally hundreds of variations, including random flashes and stripes, to create a three-dimensional display of sound.

circuitry that are linked up to carry bits of data and commands back and forth from the screen to a central point. In the case of the club, however, the monitor – strips of recessed fluorescent lighting arranged in a three-dimensional grid – is the inside of the box itself. The central point is the 'light jockey', or LJ, who is just as important as the DJ in determining the ambience. In essence, the design is a logical execution of Randolph's wish to make people 'feel as though they are inside a sound machine, a music computer, an electronic music device – seeing the music happening as it is decoded from bits to watts'. 'The sound should give form to the space and do it over time,' he adds,

'changing at each beat.' To achieve the desired impact, each evening the DJ and LJ choose one or two colours for the lighting: a palette to match the musical mood. Hard, deep techno, for instance, is rendered in minimalist whites and greens, while lighter house bathes in warmer reds and oranges. The LJ selects a range of lighting patterns from literally hundreds of variations, including random flashes and stripes, to bring the music to life in a display that makes the club synaesthetically remarkable, even for the hearing-impaired. The light grid defines the space, but capturing the most praise from visiting DJs and clubbers alike, oddly enough, are three oversized LED equalizer displays:

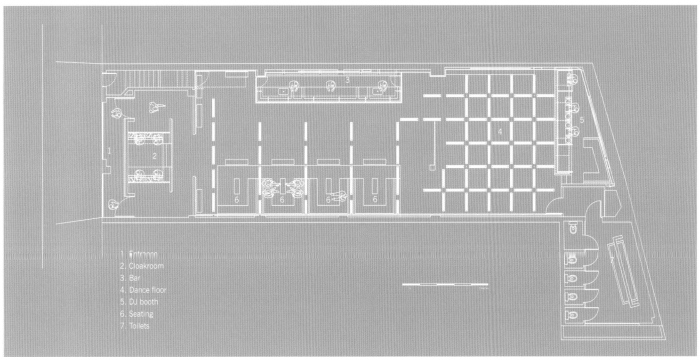

1. Entrance
2. Cloakroom
3. Bar
4. Dance floor
5. DJ booth
6. Seating
7. Toilets

The variable colour program is set each evening according to the musical mood. Harder techno takes on shades of industrial green and cold blue; lighter house music is expressed in orange or red.

behind the bar and DJ booth and on the dance-floor wall. Like the grid, these are tapped into the audio output and reflect real-time information about the sound. 'It's an obvious idea,' says Randolph, 'but it was never done before.' Randolph, a multi-talent who began his career doing graphic design for club flyers, and who has built sets for MTV Brazil as well as several fashion events, is an avid club-goer. 'I love dancing, I love music, most of my friends are DJs and I am very much involved in Brazil's electronic music scene. When I design a club space, I obviously think about how I would feel in such a space.' This reserve of personal experience gave rise to subtle touches that may go

unnoticed by the untrained eye, such as acoustically-adapted materials and the design of the DJ booth. The latter, says Randolph, 'is very comfortable and well equipped, and offers an excellent view of the whole club', all the better to maintain 'the relationship between public and DJ', which he believes is too often overlooked. 'Some booths look like cages – as if the DJ needs protection from the crowd. It's intimidating. Others are placed too far away from the dance floor, and some are too close.' At D-Edge São Paulo the DJ booth, like so many other elements, is just right.

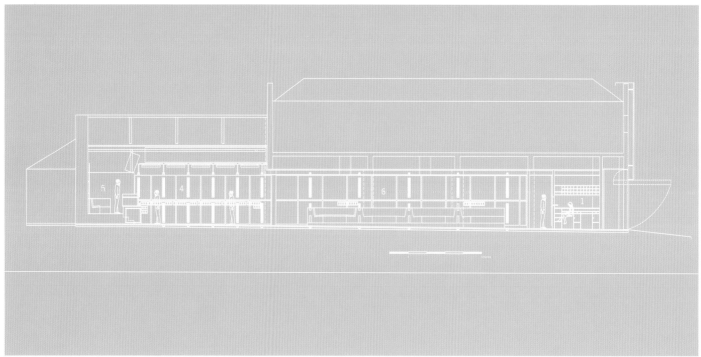

Randolph compares the interior of D-Edge to a computer; the design is a logical execution of Randolph's wish to make people 'feel as though they are inside a music computer – seeing the music happening as it is decoded from bits to watts. Most of the construction is based on black-painted wood and Plexiglas.

'I didn't think about other clubs when creating the design; I thought about computers, electronic gadgets, audio equipment and computer graphics.'

Muti Randolph

Above: The bar, to the left, is formed of 4-by-4-cm wooden rods, painted in black, and topped with glass.

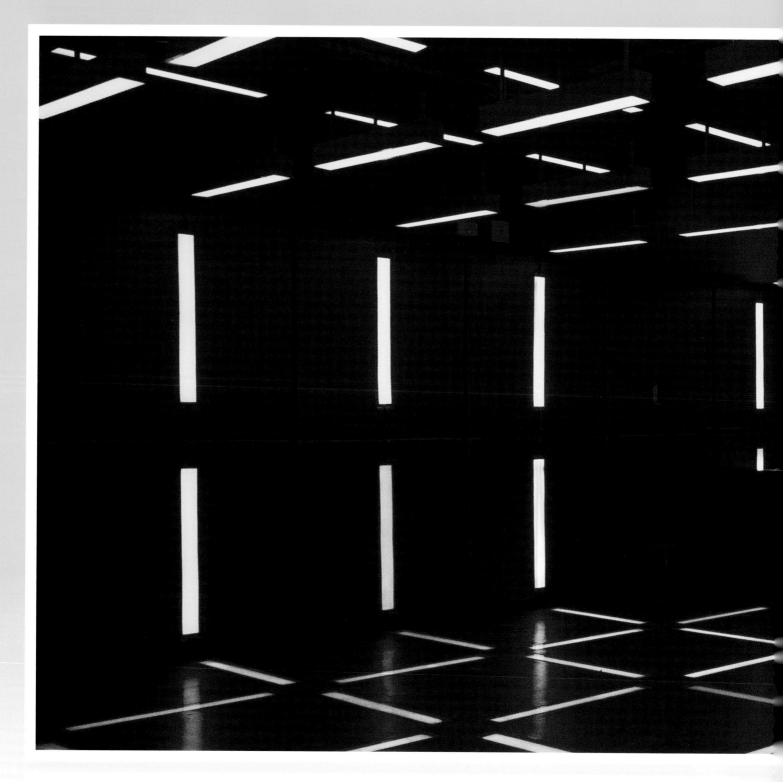

Separating the dance floor from the bar area, a dividing screen of parallel metal bars painted black repeats the stripes of the bar counter as well as wooden bars used for DJ booth and cloakroom.

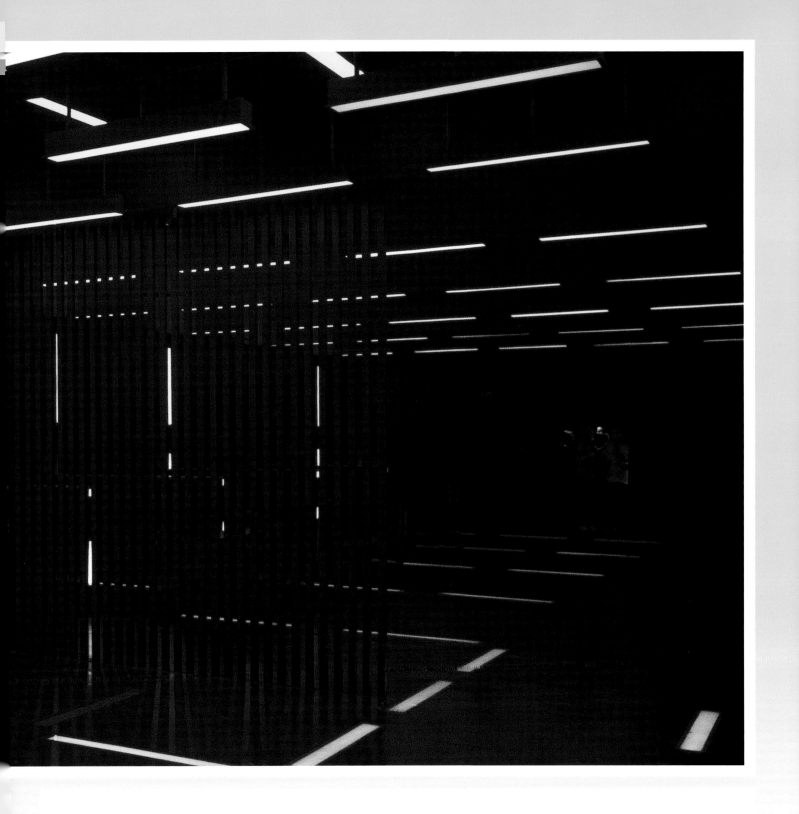

Rethinking nightlife in terms of large-scale fun, ICRAVE Design make **Crobar NY** into a mega-mecca for virtually every clubbing culture.

Only a few short years have passed since Mayor Giuliani's city-wide crackdown on club crime and the downfall of Peter Gatien's empire, which included monoliths such as Limelight, Tunnel and Club USA. Yet suddenly the 'mega-club' is resurfacing in New York City as a brand-new concept. Having risen from the rubble, clubs like Crobar's New York branch are restoring something that had recently gone missing from the Big Apple's night scene: size. With a 930-square-metre Main Room capped by nearly 20-metre-high ceilings and fitted with a top-flight sound system, Crobar NY puts the 'mega' back into mega-club. Coming from the latest addition to the Crobar family,

following the massive success of Crobars in Chicago and Miami, anything less would have been a disappointment. 'The space was formerly an old mill and forging factory in Chelsea, and it just begged to be a club,' says Lionel Ohayon, founder of ICRAVE Design, the firm contracted to create the space. 'We really wanted to bring back the idea of the big New York club, which hadn't existed for a while. One of Crobar owners Ken Smith and Cal Fortis' main objectives, was to create a New York mecca for nightlife, uniting gay culture, straight culture, techno culture – everyone.' While the promoters are responsible for merging the various subcultures under Crobar's roof, Ohayon's

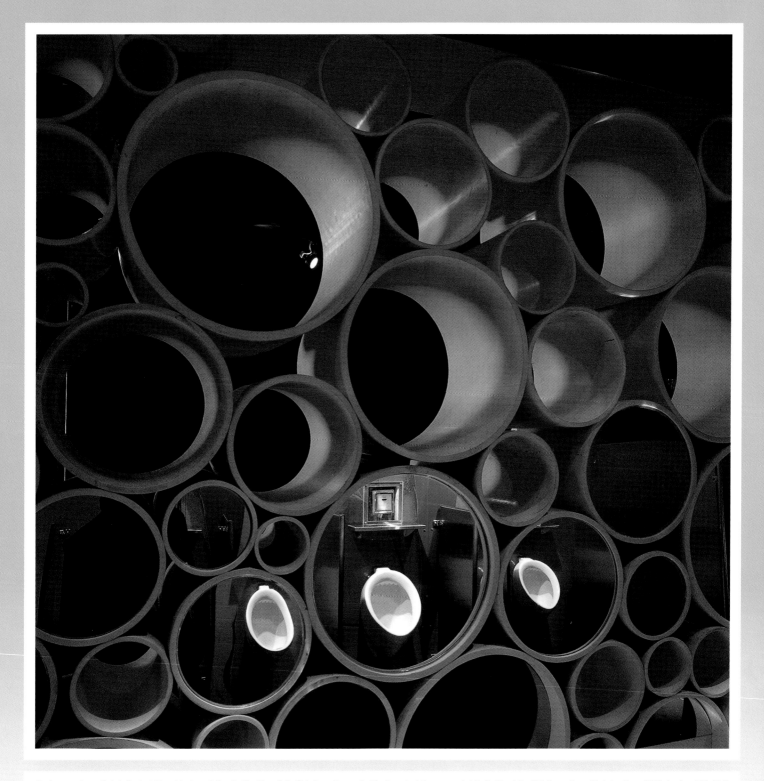

Previous page: Icrave Design's illuminated tunnel leads guests from the Reed Room to the Main Room, thus emphasizing by contrast the enormous height of ceilings in the Main Room. Above: Stacked sections of PVC pipes from 15 to 35.5 cm in diameter, some with mirror inserts, form the wall separating the men's rest room from the club. 'The concept was to disintegrate walls such that one can always have a connection to other spaces,' says designer Lionel Ohayon.

design ensures that the groups spill together by generating the kinds of unexpected encounters that bring people to clubs in the first place. 'My interest is in how people interact,' he says. 'I wanted to make sure the club wasn't a singular experience, but a series of events.' Event number one, in any club, involves leaving coats and bags in the cloakroom. Ohayon made a strategic decision to tuck this activity away on the second floor, forcing patrons to walk through a gallery space to reach it and reinforce the experience by creating a venue for rotating art exhibits by young New York artists. These exhibits create a moment of anticipation seldom associated with the

cloakroom experience, while reinforcing the notion that nightlife is a sensory theatre of art and expression that can involve many art forms. 'Checking your coat is never fun,' says Ohayon, explaining that Icrave's idea was 'to take it out of the club experience'.

From there, clubbers descend to the Reed Room, a sort of bar and staging area for the Main Room. An arresting esplanade of full-height glowing fibreglass columns gives the Reed Room its name and lends the interior an air of privacy mixed with openness. 'We tried to disintegrate the sense of walls. We didn't want the room to be defined by walls; instead we aimed for an

Visitors begin the evening in the Reed Room, where a dramatically-lit thicket of tall fibreglass 'reeds' mysteriously obscures views of the rest of the room.

'The space was formerly an old mill and forging factory in Chelsea, and it just begged to be a club.'

Lionel Ohayon

Ohayon explains the reeds as a strategic way of segmenting the room into smaller spaces: 'We didn't want the room to be defined by walls; instead we aimed for an appearance of layers and screens.'

appearance of layers and screens; this room is an experiment in haphazard encounter,' says Ohayon. Guests gather and converse intimately at seating areas clustered around the reeds, while never sacrificing a view of the space around them. Amorphous seating arrangements blend the borders between discrete areas, allowing guests engaging in conversation to turn and join another discussion going on behind them or to hear people talking just beyond an adjacent reed. A glowing tunnel feeds guests from the Reed Room into the Main Room. 'It's impossible to get the sense that the Main Room is so big from the street,' says Ohayon. 'We wanted to accentuate the magical monster

by creating the narrow tunnel.' The sheer size of the Main Room is impressive, but several elements keep the experience on a human scale. The most important consists of private bungalows, which overlook the dance floor from the mezzanine, and a private Penalty Box that hovers a metre off the ground next to the dance floor: areas designed for maximum visual synergy with the rest of the space.

Typical VIP areas in other clubs feature seating around tables filled with drinks, but seating here surrounds a miniature dance floor, while mezzanine seating sidles up to the glass balustrade. Instead of being cut off from the

The impressive Main Room is bordered on the left by the Prop Room, for VIPs. A photocell glass wall, which overlooks the Main Room dance floor, can become opaque when the room is not in use or when 'a more exclusive space' is desired.

action, VIP guests are part of what is happening in the room. Boundaries between the individual bungalows and VIP seating areas also overlap, encouraging crossovers between groups, a situation that extends to the spacious, copper-ceilinged Prop Room, also reserved for VIPs.

Fronting the dance floor is a large photocell glass wall that gives the two rooms a reciprocal vibe. (The wall is switched to opaque when the Main Room is closed.) Says Ohayon, 'It's really feeding energy off of the Main Room. The whole Prop Room is animated by how the Main Room is doing. The club wouldn't be fun unless it was fun everywhere.'

In the Prop Room, a curved copper leaf ceiling is interrupted by oval cut-outs that create private dace areas behind VIP table areas creating a multi-tiered and intimate setting for the club's VIP patrons.

The sheer size of the Main Room is impressive, but several elements keep the experience on a human scale.

A view from the top of the Grand Staircase. Doubling as a multi level dance area the Grand Staircase was designed 3 metres wide to avoid create a negative transitional space. This area carries the energy from the main level to mezzanine ensuring that people feel connected upstairs.

Giving each room a self-contained interior theme, munge//leung turns **Guvernment** into Toronto's hottest after-dark destination.

Towards the outskirts of Toronto, as the urban centre of town gives way to the former industrial harbour-front area, lies Guvernment. Unlike clubs that rely on foot traffic and nearby bars and nightlife to provide streams of up-for-it patrons, Guvernment is its own destination, drawing thousands of clubbers every weekend to its self-termed 'entertainment complex' to partake in nightly offerings in a rabbit warren of rooms as varied as the population itself. A local outfit, munge//leung: design associates, began work on the complex more than half a decade ago, and they are still at it. Beginning with smaller projects, including renovations of the Orange Room and the rooftop Sky Bar, the firm has proceeded over the years, metre by metre and room by room, to redesign the entire complex, including (chronologically) Kool Haus, the main room (called The Guvernment), the Gold Club Lounge, the Drink, Tanja, and Charlie's. And with the first wave of projects now nearly six years old – ancient by club standards – they are starting all over again. As the names suggest, each room possesses an individual personality and a self-contained interior theme. The main room, for example, is a techno-lover's paradise; the Orange Room is campy and intimate; the Drink is slick and swanky; and the Sky Bar offers Canada's jet set some terrific views of the city. Although connected to

Previous page: The outdoor Sky Bar, with expansive views of the surrounding city, features weather-resistant deck furniture and polished concrete underfoot. Above: The grey-stuccoed frame exterior of the Kool Haus features a large acrylic panel that changes colours and picks up projections, attracting notice from the street when the club is open. A sturdy corrugated-aluminium base is tough enough to survive the rowdy crowds outside.

Whereas other clubs may talk about trying to attract all types of guests on any given night, this clubbing Disneyland actually does.

Left: The palette and silky textures of The Drink create a sexy vibe, topped off with erotic poetry and images. Top right: A wavy acrylic-panelled element overhead ushers guests into the space, while concealing a projection unit above that beams images onto the adjacent wall. Above right: Toilets, accessed from the main room, pair dark cobalt-blue ceramic fixtures with red vinyl floor tiles, deep-red ceilings and stall partitions for, in Munge's words, an 'energetic and slick modern look'.

one another inside the complex, the rooms maintain separate street-linked entrances. This arrangement allows the complex to execute a unique strategy: each room can be individually marketed and promoted to a target audience for smaller events, while the club as a whole provides a coherent space for larger events. Thus, on some nights, concerts by acts ranging from The Rolling Stones to Tricky rock Kool Haus, a gay soiree swings in the Orange Room and a company throws a private party in the Sky Bar. On other nights, such as the monthly Spin, the club unites: The Guvernment and Kool Haus feature top-bill DJs like Seb Fontaine and the Crystal Method, while the Drink and the Orange Room

play R&B and deep house, leaving Charlie's and Tanja to host breakbeat and chill-out DJs. Apart from special concert events, one ticket usually provides access to the entire club. As a result, clubbers wander in awe through doors and hallways, visiting various venues, absorbing different flavours and vibes. This results in unusual mixtures: club kids, mature VIPs and artsy types may mingle in The Drink, as a more reserved crowd migrates to Charlie's and Tanja. Whereas other clubs may talk about trying to attract all types of guests on any given night, this clubbing Disneyland actually does. Alessandro Munge, who along with partner Sai Leung has seen his reputation grow with the success of

Lighting the outdoor Sky Bar was a challenge that munge//leung solved by installing several freestanding 'light pods', such as these two bracketing the illuminated bar. Says Munge: 'The advantage here is that the illumination always occurs at face level, which helps people see each other, especially when mingling. Translucent fibreglass bar fronts enhance the lightness and glow of the space.'

the club, credits owner Charles Khabouth with doing the right research and having the right instincts to pull off his vision: 'He has studied his audience well enough to cater to any age group, any culture, any preference.' And though they know their competition, Munge and Khabouth are not imitators. Having scouted their share of nightclubs to see what else is out there, they do not borrow their ideas from such venues. 'We look at art, computers, design and fashion magazines... but we try not to draw inspiration from other nightclubs. Maybe the concept of different rooms is inspired by places like the Tunnel [a former New York club], but the actual design – not so much.' In fact, the breadth of influences

is immediately evident after one glance at the cool urban-industrial sheen of Kool Haus, the Arabian pleasure-tent atmosphere of Tanja, the Art-Deco suavity of Charlie's and the Miami Beach palette of the Sky Bar. These radically different approaches have benefited from Guvernment's together-but-separate arrangement, which calls for no continuity between spaces. Furthermore, the layout has allowed for totally distinct construction budgets and timelines, as each area can be closed independently without detriment to the club as a whole. It's a formula that – given the sheer amount of space, investment and time required to set it up – seems unlikely to be challenged in Toronto, or anywhere else, for a good while to come.

LEDs and lasers draw attention to the DJ booth in the main room (called The Guvernment). 'The DJ is the Mecca of the room. Everybody dances towards him; everybody bows to him,' says Munge. 'He has become the feature.'

Each room can be individually marketed and promoted to a target audience for smaller events, while the club as a whole provides a coherent space for larger events.

The completely enclosed, 186-square-metre Gold Club Lounge overlooks the dance floor of the main room. Inspired by a product package, the designers applied hexagonal forms to give the space a distinctive look. 'It was the client's opportunity to hit a more sophisticated market,' says Munge. The designers gave it the look of luxury with a black and gold palette, while toying with softened corners and edges.

According to Munge, the team used black in the Gold Club Lounge to crank up the sex appeal, whereas gold enhances the 'underlying Gucci feel'. As he puts it, 'Gold is a bit cheesy, but it's balanced off by the modern shapes and by all of the black surrounding it.'

Against the backdrop of Caracas, Morasso Architects created **Loft**, a vaulted space that gives clubbers the illusion of floating on air.

For an architect like Juan Ignacio Morasso Tucker, who envisioned 'a space where people could feel as if they were floating on air', there could be no better commission than a nightclub in a vaulted interior with a ceiling open to the stars. This is exactly what Morasso Tucker got when a prime location under the arched rooftop of Caracas's San Ignacio Centre became available, and development group AKT 27 asked the Venezuelan architect to create the crowning glory of the shopping and entertainment complex. Morasso Tucker's skyward vision became Loft, an open-air dancing and dining venue that sets retro space-age design against a stunning backdrop of panoramic views of the surrounding city, visible from every point within. Entering the space, one abandons all thoughts of 'loft' as an architectural term and shifts to the concept of 'loft' as a verb, for the club virtually tosses visitors into midair above Caracas, enveloping them in the uninterrupted sweep of cityscape and nearby Mount Avila. The magic relies on Morasso's hanging garden of suspended tables tucked under a steel and polycarbonate canopy roof, which opens automatically in clement weather – that is to say, most of the time. In less favourable conditions, the overhead view is no less engrossing, as the roof becomes a backdrop for graphics and images projected from below.

Previous page: Thirteen circular tables suspended from a concrete pergola are featured at Loft, a restaurant and nightclub that makes great use of a spectacular open-air space. Above: The sensation of lightness is carried through to the materials, notably the perforated floors of the suspended areas. These allow for unobstructed views of the disco below, where gyrating clubbers enjoy the heady sensation of dancing under the night-time sky.

Dynamic shapes and cutouts on the entry floor offer neon-bright, distinctly Latin contrast points to the largely cooler-coloured skies framing the space.

Above left: A system of suspended catwalks and ladders links the hanging tables together. According to the designer, ventilation was achieved 'entirely by natural means'. Top right: Loft is tucked beneath the 320-square-metre steel and polycarbonate canopy roof of Caracas's San Ignacio Centre. Bottom right: The roof slides open in clement weather – that is, most of the time. In less favourable conditions, the roof still provides a spectacular view, as it becomes the backdrop for graphic projections.

Although the visitor's attention is immediately whisked up and out, Loft's interior does more than play a quiet second fiddle to the outward views. Dynamic shapes and cutouts on the entry floor, with its two bars, kitchen and lounge area, offer neon-bright, distinctly Latin contrast points to the largely cooler-coloured skies framing the space. In his palette and language of form, the architect carries out what he refers to as a 'vision of retro-futuristic inspiration, with touches of the '60s and a tinge of the European vanguard'. It is here that Morasso Tucker's influences – the designer mentions Ron Arad, Herzog & de Meuron and Toyo Ito – become visible, though Morasso's

playfulness neutralizes any monumentality or starkness that might be associated with the work of the designers he names. Morasso Tucker also acknowledges two artists for inspiring certain aspects of Loft: Venezuelan kinetic artist Jesus Soto, whose 'chromatic spaces' drove Morasso's creation of Loft's red and blue rest rooms; and Alexander Calder, whose bold sculptures are mimicked by rubber shapes floating above the dance floor. Morasso Tucker's Calder-like 'clouds' are more than an aesthetic addition to the club; they also serve an important acoustic function in the roofless space. Much of the existing structure of the building was assimilated into, and even

Top and above left: All furniture was purpose-designed by Morasso Tucker, including modular seating and a room-length, cut-out light sculpture, both located in the lounge. Right: Loft guests are treated to the balmy Caracas air, as well as to great views of the surrounding city and nearby Mount Avila.

emphasized by, the architecture of Morasso Tucker. Access to the space is controlled at the opposite side of San Ignacio Centre's galleria. Having queued and paid, visitors traverse a narrow catwalk that foreshadows a network of suspended paths interconnecting tables above the dance floor. Guests cross the atrium to enter Loft. Hanging from a concrete pergola, the tables incorporate several trusses that support the building. Rings wrapped around large, load-bearing concrete columns serve as drink stands at ground level and as lighting above. Morasso Tucker also capitalized on the intrinsic properties of the space to ventilate the venue. As he explains, 'The ventilation is entirely by

natural means. The flow of air that circulates through the different openings located on top, as well as on some sides, of the disco prevents the potential accumulation of smoke and heat, even with a large number of visitors.' Morasso Tucker wove the sensation of open air and circulation through the materials as well. Highlighting the project, in terms of materials and visual impact, are leather, illuminated surfaces and an effect of transparency. In aiming for a totally integrated space, he used 'the sensation of lightness, as well as indirect light, to achieve an illusion of sensuality, of that which is hidden'. The implementation of these goals is most notable in the perforated

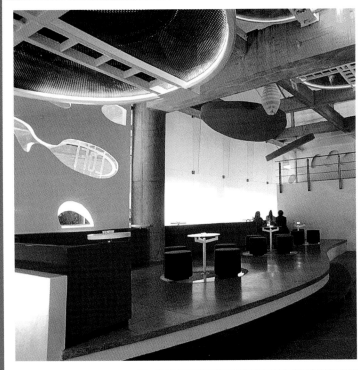

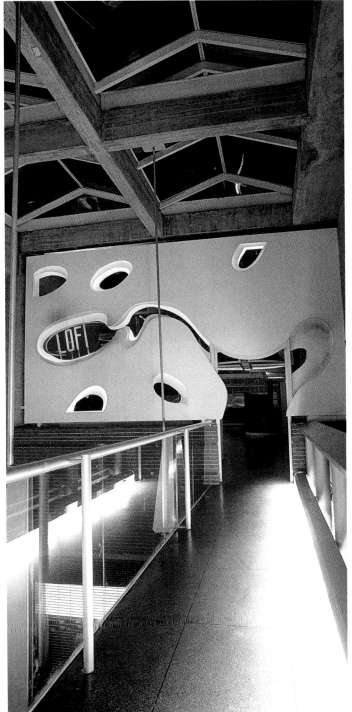

Top and above left: Playful lighting blends the different levels together, adding dashes of colour throughout the patron's field of vision. Right: Visitors to Loft enter via a catwalk which crosses the atrium of the San Ignacio Centre, warming them up to the network of suspended catwalks that make up a large part of the club's interior.

metal floors that serve the suspended tables. Ringed with neon below, these elements appear light and do not obstruct the view above. The combination of style and scenery transports visitors, while visually scrambling their reference points to time and space. The completed project reminds Morasso Tucker 'of the Jetson family', and he imagines visitors 'looking for a small spacecraft that carries and drops off young party-goers'.

Top: At ground-floor level are two bars, each stretching 12 metres in length. Their indirect lighting, concealed behind metal elements, 'creates an illusion of sensuality and transparency', says Morasso Tucker, who transformed certain existing components, such as concrete columns, into drink stands and other functional features. Bottom left: Morasso Tucker refers to rubber shapes floating above the dance floor and lounge as 'clouds'. References to the work of Alexander Calder,

Reminded of the Jetson family, architect Juan Morasso Tucker imagines visitors 'looking for a small spacecraft that carries and drops off young party-goers'.

these visual enhancements double as acoustic aids in the open-air space. Opposite page, bottom right: The women's rest room, finished in red, draws inspiration from the 'chromatic spaces' of Venezuelan kinetic artist Jesus Soto. Blue was chosen for the men's room. This page: The lightness and translucence of the materials, along with the repetition of rings of light from floor to ceiling, unite the various areas of Loft into 'one big common space', in the words of Morasso Tucker.

Working the old into the new, d-ash design transforms **The Spider Club** into a highly detailed and luxurious members-only lounge in New York City.

At the time designer David Ashen received the commission to create The Spider Club, in an unrenovated attic space hidden away in the upper reaches of the newly refurbished New York club Avalon, coincidence had it that he was in the midst of another project nearby. 'I was doing a kindergarten down the street, a block away from Spider,' says Ashen. 'One was a playground for children and the other a playground for adults.' Though their functions are different, Ashen sees a surprising similarity in the two venues. 'It's all fantasy,' he says. Ashen had already indulged his playground fantasy, which has myriad forms, while redesigning Avalon, formerly the Limelight, one of the gravitational centres of

New York's legendary club scene in the '80s and '90s. Avalon's new owners had recently acquired a club in Los Angeles, which became the first Spider Club, an exclusive members-only lounge. Eager to introduce the successful model in New York, which would replicate everything from the selective membership programme to the Moroccan details of the L.A. club, they recruited Ashen to do it. Made up of two modest adjoining rooms, the Spider Club-to-be had previously hosted a Gothic 'S/M Night' (Ashen's team removed the chains from the wall) and a 'back room' and had been, most recently, a derelict storage space within Avalon – each incarnation's sordid history and residue stood in stark contrast to

Previous page: Echoing its sister club in Los Angeles, the New York Spider Club pays homage to Moroccan interiors. 'We brought in mirrors and coin skirts, among other things,' says designer David Ashen, 'and put them on the walls to create a texture.' The pop colours and crisp forms of the Tube Lounge, in the background, are a contrast to this theme. Above: From a low-profile door on an alley next to the refurbished Avalon, members enter the tunnel

the high detail and luxury envisioned for the Spider Club. As he had done in transforming the Limelight, Ashen paid strict attention to the surfaces and the architectural bones of the interior. 'We were playing with the dialogue between the new and the old,' he says, stressing the use of 'sleek and expressive skins'. Working the old into the new, Ashen's team closed off the windows surrounding the walls of the Main Lounge with acrylic resin backed with colour-changing LED lighting. Hues from the warm lighting swirl into a ruddy palette composed of 'maroon red and chocolate brown, layered in blues and reds'. Thanks to these earthy tones, the unlikely bedfellows of Moroccan furnishings and Gothic

architecture seem happily at ease in the Main Lounge. Rather than clumsily transplanting pieces from a Bedouin tent, Ashen expressed the Moroccan theme by introducing a subtle interplay of elements and sensations. 'We brought in mirrors and coin skirts, among other things,' he says, 'and put them on the walls to create a texture'. Ashen's cocktail tables include silver Moroccan tea trays mounted on legs, which he paired with square, aluminium-legged walnut tables. Echoing the mix of cocktail tables, intricate Moroccan details are combined with bolder, simpler, contemporary elements to strike the right note. Above the dance floor, a cluster of mirrored disco balls adds a layer of glitter and texture to the

to The Spider Club. 'There's an air of mystery,' Ashen says. Plastic grass – 'for texture' – and climbing plants adorn the wall. This page, top: Punched-metal lanterns lead the way to the club's location in the attic of Avalon. Above: Ashen's team closed off the Gothic windows of the Main Lounge with acrylic resin backed with colour-changing LEDs. The warm colours swirl into a palette of 'maroon red and chocolate brown, layered in blues and reds'.

space. 'We grouped them so that, when lit in the right way, they look like crystal balls,' says the designer, who wanted 'to create another decorative plane'. The Tube Lounge, in the adjoining room, is a world away from the swanky, low-lit Main Lounge. The upholstered tubular room is capped at one end by a double wall of glass, with LED lighting behind and primary-coloured vinyl dots in front. According to Ashen, the bright light and glass walls make clubbers feel as though they are 'sitting in a museum box'. He repeated the pop colours of the wall in tables fashioned from yellow, orange and red plastic laminates. Like the Main Lounge, the Tube Lounge is intimate, but unlike many VIP-orientated

spaces, neither offers places to hide. Owing to a strict membership-only policy, an unmarked entrance on a side street, and a seemingly secluded attic space, which can be accessed only by ascending several flights of stairs, visitors to the Spider Club feel secure and can let down their guard. Taking advantage of these elements, Ashen's team built platforms into the space that function as vantage points, and employed low cushions to divide the couches. Thanks to a ruddy palette composed of 'maroon red and chocolate brown, layered in blues and reds', the unlikely bedfellows of Moroccan furnishings and Gothic architecture seem happily at ease in the Main Lounge.

Slick painted each room in Chicago's **Sound-Bar** a different vibrant colour, creating a rhythm of movement that surprises patrons at every turn.

The earliest roots of house music lie deep within Chicago, offshoots of early New York disco and top Chicago DJs such as Frank Knuckles, Derrick Carter and Jeff Mills have long toured the world as headliners. Given this, one might expect Chicago's club scene to have achieved equal renown. But this has not been the case, claims Rocco Laudizio, founder and principal of Slick Design and Manufacturing. 'Chicago is a great city,' he says, 'but in the nightclub and lounge scene, nobody was spending money or doing anything creative.' To fill this perceived design void, Laudizio and his team created popular venues - Nine, Ghost Bar, Y Bar, Syn, Wet and Spybar - for various

clients. And when long-standing nightlife entrepreneurs Stefan Billen and Mark Jurczyk needed someone to design their dream project, Slick knew they could make room for one more. 'Sound-Bar is so high level, so ultimate,' says Laudizio, patently enthusiastic about 'dancing, lounging and VIPing all under one roof'. 'It has the details of restaurants in New York – that level of finish had never been done in Chicago. Five years ago it was unheard of, except for maybe in a few hotel bars.'Laudizio is fanatical about colour, a passion he traces back to comic-strip heroes that featured in the TV shows he loved as a child. 'Growing up, I was a big fan of Green Hornet

Previous page: Slick Design principal Rocco Laudizio credits a childhood fascination with superhero comics as the source of his love for the intensely saturated colours that define the club. VIPs use a special lift near the club's entrance to access the Green Room downstairs. Above: The colourful spaces of the lower level – the Red Room (pictured here), Green Room and Orange Room follow uniform plans and share details. In each room, a back wall of white metallic

'Sound-Bar has the details of restaurants in New York – that level of finish had never been done in Chicago.'

Rocco Laudizio

laminate bounces brightly tinted light around the space. Bar fronts are chrome with acrylic portholes, and custom furniture is upholstered to match each space. This page, left: Slick Design's signature Lollipop table was used throughout the club for its versatility. In the Red Room, red-acrylic tabletops are attached (by a single hex-head screw) to red powder-coated aluminium bases. Right: Mosaic accents in the Red Room and other areas are the work of Italian craftsmen.

and Batman. I loved the vibrant colours in those productions.' He told Billen and Jurczyk that he 'wanted do each room in an individual colour'. Laudizio's team combed through samples looking for the right shades of orange, green, red and blue to bring each space to life. These vivid shades are wrapped in a relatively low-key exterior, the dock of a warehouse, which is practically the only element left unfinished in the Sound-Bar experience. In fact, Slick even enhanced the wear and rust on the landing dock to make it look older, thereby setting up visitors for an even bigger shock as they enter the super-refined interior. Once they're inside, says Laudizio, 'People

freak! As soon as they walk in, it's like, "Oh my god!" Inside, elite guests are immediately whisked downstairs – via an exclusive lift – to the VIP room, leaving everyone else to queue for the coat check. The Entrance Bar area, crafted in rich chocolate ash panelling with an Amber glowing acrylic bar front, is the first hint of the extensive colour-theming to follow. Laudizio and his team planned the visitor's first steps into Sound-Bar with careful precision: 'We created a rhythm of movement that would keep you surprised around every corner. We didn't want dance floor or the Round Bar VIP room visible when you walk in. You're about 30 metres into the space.

Left: Booth seating in the maroon round VIP bar on the entry floor is set in front of fabric-covered wall panels; fabric-clad foam balls above the seating echo circular portholes on bar fronts and partitions. Right: Made from high-polished chrome laminate, the DJ booth, with its six turntables, can accommodate two DJs simultaneously. Opposite page, left: The Orange Room follows the uniform plan designed for the lower level, which called for sofas to be clad in vinyl for durability.

You've already seen so much... and then you see the dance floor, and it's like an explosion.' Colours dazzle on the 4-by-6-metre video walls facing the dance floor. Six-meter-tall glass partitions offer an escape route to the bar when the dance floor is in full swing. Nearby, pulsating monitors and lights draw visitors to the LED video waterfall at the main staircase leading guests to the lower level. Roy G. Biv would be right at home on the lower level, faced with the cheerful choice of Red Room, Orange Room or Green Room (the elusive VIP zone). Although the colours may be spectral opposites, the execution is consistent.

In each room, a back wall of white metallic laminate bounces brightly tinted light around the space, teaming with coloured acrylic, stainless steel and chrome used in the bars to create and deflect intensely coloured light. Each piece of furniture has been custom designed and made by Slick, to match the room in question, and carefully selected fabrics harmonize perfectly with wall colours. 'It's *that* close,' says Laudizio about the exacting detail. 'That's how crazy we were.' After the completed interior sat behind closed doors in permit purgatory for more than a year, Sound-Bar finally seems to have achieved the success destined for it, at least according to

The design team painstakingly matched all fabrics to the colours used in the three rooms on this floor. Top right: The distinctive round VIP bar in the Maroon Room has a chrome front with cutouts backed by illuminated acrylic. The room boasts an impressive VIP rest room with a frosted-glass door that turns red when closed and in use. Above right: Sound-Bar's vibrantly coloured rooms (pictured is the Orange Room) and refined finishes make it a standout in Chicago.

sales figures and reviews. Laudizio, however, relies on another statistic: 'The way I knew it was a design success was that everyone walked in and right away got on their cell phones to call friends', it's a phenomenon that takes the phrase 'word of mouth' to a whole new level.

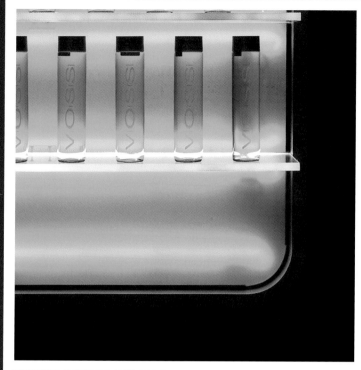

Top left: The detail of the back-bar display cabinet on the dance floor reveals a custom aluminium frame with blue and frosted white shelves that match the blue theme of the dance floor. Above left: A VIP seating level overlooks the dance floor. The glass railing system was custom designed for this area, and colour-changing blue vinyl covers the booths.

The dance floor is ablaze with dynamic images and colours. Video walls, measuring about 4 x 6 metres, face the dance floor, and 6-metre-tall glass partitions offer an escape route to the bar when the dance floor is in full swing, along with custom made and formed white acrylic column covers that contain LED lightning to change with the music beats.

A new club or an actual person? Graham Downes Architecture set out to take clubbers on a voyage through the anatomy of San Diego's **Thin**.

'I am a visual being,' proclaims the website for San Diego's Thin, 'thinking in pictures, spaces, traveling effortlessly. Transformation is fortuitous. Memories created in the moment, experienced, stored in the anatomy of time.' It's unclear whether the message is intended to reflect the mantras of the target group for whom this hip new lounge is intended, or whether Thin itself is speaking in the first person. Either way, the small space, located in a historic building in San Diego's Gaslamp District, commands a presence strong enough to lend credibility to this lyrical persona.

Thin picked up its moniker during the early phases of the project, which called for a division of the 13-by-33-metre space and the subsequent creation of a public bar down the length of one side and a private-event space on the other. 'We wanted a bar that wasn't going to feel empty,' explains Graham Downes, principal of Graham Downes Architecture, the team behind the design project. 'But that premise didn't last long.' Yet Downes and his team held on to the name and began to riff on its less literal applications to the space. 'Thin is about the fragility of membranes and transparency of layers,' says the designer.

Previous page:Thin strips of ebony flooring and a Plexiglas light box over the bar emphasize the length and narrowness of the slender space. Above: Play, a VIP lounge space at one end of the club, is cordoned off by two sets of curtains on circular tracks.

The devices employed by Downes to demarcate the different areas are, indeed, nearly diaphanous. The heaviest is the circular curtain separating Thin from Play, the private lounge area contained in the space once earmarked for a restaurant. 'Separating Play is a highly reflective vinyl curtain, made from the same material as firemen's outfits,' says Downes. 'It reflects all the light from the street. Streaming white and red lights create a running light show on the reflective grey material.' The whole arrangement hangs several centimetres above the ground, hardly an impermeable division. Another curtain, this one orange, hangs just inside the reflective one, which is staggered slightly higher

to reveal a shock of danger orange that is visible from the bar. Opening these curtains fuses Play and Thin into one space. The divisions between areas within Thin are even less substantial. Another curtain can be extended from the entry down the length of the lounge to further carve up the space. A bar runs lengthwise along one side of the long corridor. A row of armless banquettes, separated by white, powder-coated-metal drink tables, folded down from wall consoles, lines the other side. Between these are two lengthwise arrangements of custom-created and shaped stainless-steel drink-stand and seating elements, each affixed to the ceiling by stainless-steel poles,

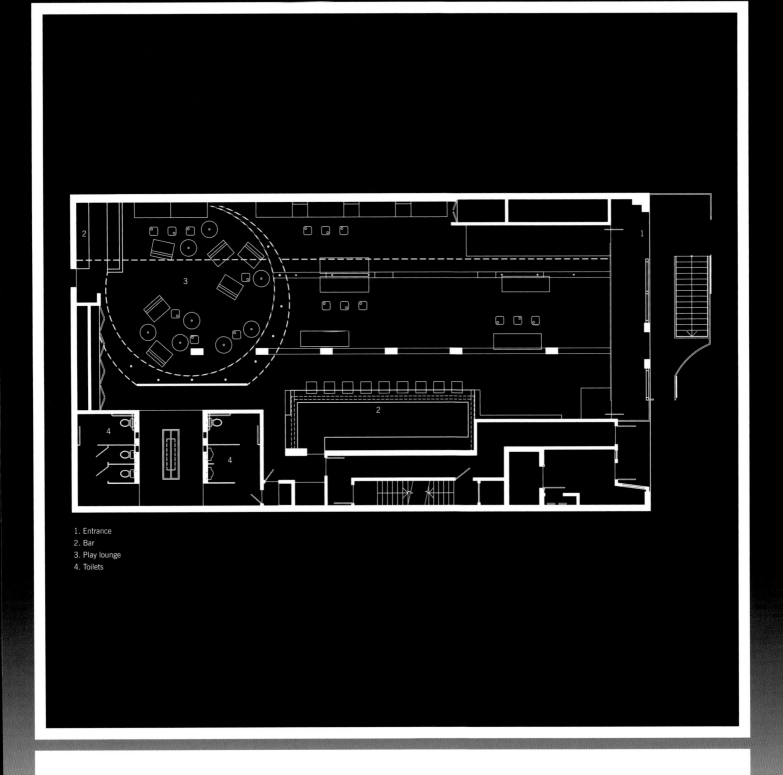

1. Entrance
2. Bar
3. Play lounge
4. Toilets

'Thin is about the fragility of membranes and transparency of layers.'

Graham Downes

Top left: Graham Downes Architecture's purpose-designed tables boast recesses for glasses. These white fibreglass tables are sturdy enough to double as seats. Top and bottom right: Graham Downes collaborated with graphic-design firm Pool to craft the distinctive visual system of the bar, which blends travel and medical references. Bottom left: Lining one side of the space is a row of armless banquettes separated by white powder-coated metal drink

The graphic reference to the clinic is one of many that blend with travel imagery to create Thin's unique pictorial and graphic language.

tables. Taking their cue from the travel metaphor, the tables fold down from wall consoles. Above: In the rest room, crisp fluorescent lighting, white tiles, and a steel dissecting table create a startlingly clinical atmosphere. 'The way that doctors and surgeons look at people is almost mechanical,' says principal Graham Downes, adding that 'we weren't trying to shock'.

a reference, Downes explains, to the poles in burlesque shows. The partition used to section off the bathroom area is a translucent glass panel clad in a frosted film bearing enlarged images of doctors' prescription-pad scrawls. This graphic reference to the clinic is one of many that blend with travel imagery to create Thin's unique pictorial and graphic language, described by Downes as 'a voyage through anatomy'. Above the banquettes, a light box runs the length of the wall with, Downes says, 'a continuous band of images of different cell structures coming from human matter – all different things, including diseased and normal tissues'.

The sink in the bathroom was modelled on a dissecting table, with tiles and crisp fluorescent lighting to match. 'The way that doctors and surgeons look at people is almost mechanical. We weren't trying to shock, but we wanted to cut back on the quality of light for the stainless-steel cadaver-laboratory sink.' The travel metaphor is most visible in the fold-down trays between the banquettes, as well as the continuous line of the backrest, which Downes compares to airports and train stations. 'You sit temporarily; it's a short space while you're in transit. It's temporary in your life and temporary in your evening.'

'Thin is about the fragility of membranes and transparency of layers,' says Downes.

Downes admits that the transitory styling of the furniture is also intended to 'make people feel a little uncomfortable', which, in this case, is not a bad thing. 'It's kind of the point to "move their cheese". They have to cross the room at the beginning of evening, when the space is empty, to walk to the bar, which makes them both more visible and more vulnerable. It disorients them a little bit.' In Downes's mind, it is this disorientation that leads to the interesting confrontations that get people to go out in the first place and that keep them coming back.

Academy (14-21)
Bunda Street
Canberry
Australia
T +61 2 6257 3355
info@academyclub.com.au
www.academyclub.com.au
Open: 5 pm-late Thu-Fri

Client: Club Academy
Interior architect: SJB Interiors
Design team: Bo Christensen,
Megan Hounslow, Andrew Parr
(principal), Robert Saggni,
Radka Syrova
General contractor: Crown Projects
Manufacturers: Cattelani & Smith,
Cite, DeDeCe, Décor Pebble,
Di Emme Creative Solutions,
Pillkington, Rimex
Max. capacity: 610
Total floor area (m²): 700
Total cost (€): 1,420,000
Budget per m² (€): 2028
Duration of construction: 6 months
Opening: 27 January 2004
Photography: Tony Miller

ABSOLUT ICEBAR (86-93)
At the Icehotel
98191 Jukkasjärvi
Sweden
T +46 980 66800
F +46 980 66890
info@icehotel.com

www.icehotel.com
Open: 1 pm-1 am Mon-Sun (11
December-mid April)
Dress code: Warm clothing

Interior architects:
Arne Bergh and Åke Larsson
General contractor: Icehotel
Consultants: Icehotel
Engineers: Icehotel
Manufacturers: Icehotel
Capacity: 200
Total floor area (m²): 200
Duration of construction: 2 weeks
Opening: 11 December 2004

Babushka (234-241)
2a the Printworks, Withy Grove
Manchester M4 2BS
England
T +44 161 8321 234
babushkamanchester@
styleinthecity.co.uk
www.styleinthecity.co.uk
Open: 5 pm-4 am Wed-Sun
Music: Disco, funk, soul,
progressive house, R&B
Dress code: Smart

Client: Babushka
Interior architect: Lief Design
General contractor:
Daleside Shopfitters
Consultants: Lief Design
(lighting), E&L Chambers,

Tarsins (74, 74) (decoration)
Engineers: CSW (heating
and ventilation)
Manufacturers: B-Lux,
Boss Design, Café Interiors,
Catellan Italia, HB Design,
Johanson design, Medessin,
Morris Furniture, Moooi
Max. capacity: 800
Total floor area (m²): 1000
Total cost (£): 250,000
Budget per m² (£): 250
Duration of construction: 6 weeks
Opening: 18 September 2003
Photography: Laurence Hudghton

BarRouge (126-133)
Messeplatz 10, Level 31
4058 Basel
Switzerland
T +41 61 3611 031
reservation@barrouge.ch
www.barrouge.ch
Open: 5 pm-1 am Mon-Wed; 5
pm-2 am Thu; 5 pm-4 am Fri-Sat;
8 pm-1 am Sun
Music: House, R&B, salsa
Dress code: No white socks

Client: BR Basel
Interior architect and design team:
Holzer Kobler Architekturen
Consultants: Bernd Altenried
(wood), Rolf Derrer (lighting),
Tod Hanson (artwork walls and

ceiling), R+B Engineering
(electrical)
Engineers: Anton Riesen
(sanitary), Techdata (coordination),
Thieme Klima (ventilation),
Walther Mory Maier Bauingenieure
(civil), ZZ (gastronomy)
Manufacturers: A. Steiner
(bar and seating), Di Legno (floor),
Lienert Caviola (sanitary)
Max. capacity: 350
Total floor area (m²): 350
Total cost (€): 1,000,000
Budget per m² (€): 2850
Duration of construction: 8 weeks
Opening: 12 December 2003
Photography: Francisco Carrascosa

Bed Supperclub (38-45)
26 Soi Sukhumvit 11
Sukhumvit Road, Klongtoey-Nua,
Wattana
Bangkok 10110
Thailand
T +66 2 6513 537
www.bedsupperclub.com
Open: 7.30 pm-1.30 am Mon-Sun
Music: Hip-hop, house,
Latin dance
Dress code: Smart

Client: Oxygen Holdings
Architect and interior architect:
Orbit Design Studio
Design team: Songchai

Criavanothar, Ralph Dodd
(graphics), Simon Drogemuller
(lead interior architect),
Scott Edwards (project architect),
Putthachad Kasisedapan,
Christopher Redpath (director-in-
charge), Johnnie Searle (project
manager), Peter Tucker
(project manager)
Consultants: Groovelax (A/V),
Orbit Design (studio lighting and
A/V), Oxygen Holdings (A/V)
Engineers: Warnes Associates
(structural), EFSI (mechanical and
electrical)
Manufacturers: Orbit Design Studio
Max. capacity: 200
Max. sound levels (dB): 105
Total floor area (m²): 840
Total cost (US$): 850,000
Budget per m² (US$): 1012
Duration of construction: 8 months
Opening: September 2002
Photography: Marcus Gortz

buzADA (62-69)
Galatasaray Island Kurucesme
Istanbul
Turkey
T +90 212 2636 373
buz@veezy.com
www.buzbar.com
Open: 9 am-4 am daily
Music: House, Turkish pop
Dress code: Chic

Client: buz Group
Architect: Mahmut Anlar
Interior architect: Geomim Design
Designers: Beyza Korman, Engin
Ozmen (assistant), Nihat Sinan Erul
General contractor: Tasari Yapi
Consultants: 1e1 Design
(graphics), Geomim Design
(lighting), Telesine (sound)
Engineers: Ismail Ciceksoy (static),
Nuray Keskin (furniture),
Esat Konuk (sound),
Nimet Tanriverdi (construction)
Manufacturers: Imaj Textile,
Masif Furniture, Monte Carlo Tents
Max. capacity: 3500
Total floor area (m²): 5500
Total cost (US$): 670,000
Budget per m² (US$): 121
Duration of construction: 45 days
Opening: 17 June 2004
Photography: Yavuz Draman

Cab (198-205)
2, place du Palais-Royal
75001 Paris
France
T +33 1 5862 5625
info@cabaret.fr
www.cabaret.fr
Open: 11.30 pm-dawn Thu-Sat
Music: Electro, hip-hop, house
Dress code: Smart

Client: Le Cabaret
Interior architect: Ora-Ïto
Design team: Ito, Nicolas
Delefosse
Engineers: Ora-Ïto
Manufacturers: La Boisserole,
De Sede, Dupont de Nemours,
Giraudon
Max. capacity: 500-600
Total floor area (m²): 500
Total cost (€): 2,000,000
Budget per m² (€): 5000
Duration of construction: 4 months
Opening: January 2003

Le Carrousel (222-225)
10, Place de la Bourse
44000 Nantes
France
T + 33 240 4819 90
antoniacarver@le-carrousel.com
www.le-carrousel.com
Open: 10 pm-4 am daily
Music: Electro, funk, house
Dress code: Fashionable

Client: BGJ
Interior architect:
Alfredo Rodriguez
Design team: Hazard Studio
General contractor:
Douaud Agencement
Consultants: Fresnel
Manufacturers: Kartell,
Melogranoblu, Soca

Max. capacity: 300
Total floor area (m²): 301
Total cost (€): 600,000
Budget per m² (€): 2000
Duration of construction: 5 months
Opening: March 2004
Photography: Stéphane Chalmeau

Cinnamon Club Bar (206-213)
The Old Westminster Library
Great Smith Street
London SW1P 3BU
England
T +44 20 7222 2555
info@cinnamonclub.com
www.cinnamonclub.com
Open: 6 pm-midnight Mon-Sat
Music: Ambient house, Indian house
Dress code: Smart

Client: Iqbal Wahhab
Interior architect: Mueller Kneer
Associates
Design team: Anne-Laure
Gimenez, Olaf Kneer (principal),
Marianne Mueller (principal)
General contractor:
Genus Property Services
Consultants: Chris Gunton
Associates (A/V)
Manufacturers: Concept Bars,
Creation Baumann, Lasar
Contracts, Walter Knoll, Rajasthan
(hand-crafted and imported furniture)
Max. capacity: 80

Total floor area (m²): 95

Total cost (£): 220,000

Budget per m² (£): 2315

Duration of construction: 3 months

Opening: May 2002

Photography: Marq Bailey,

Rolant Dafis

Coconclub (54-61)

Russia

The interior has been destroyed
by fire.

Interior architect: Savinkin/Kuzmin
project group

Design team: Dmitri Khromov,
Vladimir Kuzmin (principal), Anna
Logacheva, Anna Novoselskaja,
Vladislav Savinkin (principal),
Tatiana Tcheliapina,
Eugenia Tikhonova

Contractors: Alfa-Station
(construction, woodwork),
Bioinjector (glass, metal,
concrete), Flat Interiors (furniture)

Consultants: Light and Sound

Engineers: Liga Klimata

Manufacturers: Album, Biesse,
Bisazza, Glass, iGuzzini,
Sturm and Plastic

Max. capacity: 200-400

Total floor area (m²): 400

Total cost (US$): 2,000,000

Budget per m²: 5000

Duration of construction:

2001-2002

Opening: 2002

Photography: K. Ovchinnikov

CocoonClub (118-125)

Carl-Benz-Strasse 21

60386 Frankfurt am Main

Germany

T +49 69 5069 6948

info@cocoonclub.net

www.cocoonclub.net

Open: 9 pm-6 am Fri-Sat
(CocoonClub); 7 pm-3 am Tue-Thr;
7 pm-6 am Fri-Sat (Micro); 8 pm-
1 am Tue-Sat (Silk)

Music: Electronic

Client: Cocoon-Club

Interior architects: 3deluxe

Art Direction: Dieter Brell, Andreas
and Stephan Lauhoff, Nik Sweiger

Project Management: Peter Seipp,
Janine Schmidt

Design team: Niko Alexopoulos,
Christian Buchkremer, Joaquín
Busch, Max Diemand, Sascha
Jahnke, Michael Jancsó, Jacob
Keizer, Sascha Koeth, Markus
Pretnar, Mark Owen, Joern
Refsnaes, Mareike Reusch,
Norman Schneider, Ralph
Schöneberg, Philipp Walter

Graphics: 3deluxe

General contractor:
System Modern

Consultants: Karlen - Labor für
kinetisches licht, Lightpower,
medienproject p2, meso-digital
media system design, Screen.NT,
Teamtec Media Technology

Manufacturers: biggAIR, Bürklin,
Freiraumx, Gecco Scene
Construction, Glas Schröder,
Karlen Labor für Kinetisches Licht,
Kessler, Klunderschmid, Meso
Digital Media Systems Design,
Villa Rocca, Steelworks

Max. capacity: 1200

Total floor area (m²): 2664

Duration of construction: 8 months

Opening: July 2004

Photography: Emanuel Raab

Collage Bar (242-245)

301 Argyle Street

Glasgow G2 8DL

Scotland

T +44 141 2043 333

Open: noon-midnight Mon-Thu;
noon-1 am Fri-Sat

Client: Radisson Sas/MWB

Interior architect: Graven Images

Design team: Stephen Boyd,
Jim Hamilton, Ross Hunter,
Graeme Johnston, John Martina,
Frank McGarva, William Nolan

General contractor: Elmwood

Consultants: Graven Images,
T and A

Engineers: Blyth and Blyth

Manufacturers: Ads Sign and
Light, Alan Courtenay, Altro,
Andrew Muirhead Leather,
Bishopbriggs Upholstery,
Bibliotheque, Caldwell Wright
Ironmongery, Corian,
Craigie Carpets, Haran Glass,
Iguzzini, Jack Hogans, Parkhead
Welding, Plank, Shadbolt Veneers,
Spatial Furniture

Max. capacity: 150

Duration of construction: 12 weeks

Opening: November 2002

Photography: Keith Hunter

Crobar NY (254-261)

530 West 28th Street

New York, NY 10001

USA

T +1 212 6299 000

www.crobarnyc.com

Open: 9 pm-4 am Thu-Fri; 9 pm-5
am Sat; 9 pm-4 am Sun

Music: Progressive house

Dress code: Clean, clubby,
fun and stylish

Client: Zoom Productions

Interior architects: Big Time
Design, ICRAVE Design studio

Design team: Siobhan Barry,
Callin Fortis, Shawn Hope,
Orlando Lamas, Lionel Ohayon
(principal)

General contractor: Bond & Walsh

Consultants: Artfag (A/V),
Focus Lighting, Phazon Sound,
SJ Lighting

Engineers: Telesco Associates

Manufacturers: Ardex by Flooring
Solutions, Cascade Coil, Chicago
Faucets, Dune, Evergreen,
Fiberglass World, Forma Glas,
Formglas Canada, Hunnell Street
Tile Works, Nemo Tile, Perfect
Circle, Renewed Materials LLC,
Shaw/Young Metal Design

Max. capacity: 4000

Total floor area (m²): 20,000
over two levels

Total cost (US$): 6,000,000

Budget per m² (US$): 2200

Duration of construction: 7 months

Opening: 11 December 2003

Photography: Frank Oudeman

Culture Club (174-181)

Afrikalaan 174

9000 Ghent

Belgium

T +32 9 2676 442

info@cultureclub.be

www.cultureclub.be

Open: 11 pm-6 am Fri-Sat

Music: Electro, hip-hop, house,
R&B, reggae

Dress code: Anything from street
wear to hot couture

Client: Bel.mondo

Interior architect: Glenn Sestig
Architects

General contractor: Descamps
Decoratie

Consultants: Duncan Verstraeten
(lighting)

Engineers: D&D Architecten

Graphics: Diederik Serlet

Manufacturers: Descamps
Decoratie

Max. capacity: 1000

Total cost (€): 1,000,000

Duration of construction: 4 months

Opening: November 2002

Photography: Jean-Pierre Gabriel

D-Edge (246-253)

Alameda Olga 170

Barra Funda, São Paulo

Brazil

T +55 11 3667 8334

office@d-edge.com.br

www.d-edge.com.br

Open: 11 pm-6 am Sun-Thu;
11 pm-7 am Fri; 11 pm-12 am Sat

Music: Electro, house, progressive
house, rock, techno

Dress code: Trendy or more casual
(dress is party-related)

Client: Renato Ratier (D-Edge)

Interior architect: Muti Randolph

Design team: Carol Bueno,
Paulo Filisetti

General contractor: Triptyque

Manufacturers: Adriana Addam
(polyurethane resin), Claudio Alves
(wall cushion), Geraldo Cruz
(glass), Dmx (lighting), Silvestre de
Oliveira (wood furniture), Gilberto
dos Santos (masonry)

Max. capacity: 600

Total floor area (m²): 270

Duration of construction: 3.5
months

Opening: 22 April 2003

Photography: Rômulo Fialdini

Divina (110-117)

Via Molino delle Armi

20100 Milan

Italy

T +39 02 5843 1823

F +39 02 5843 9903

info@divina.biz

www.divina.biz

Client: Bunko

Interior architect: Fabio Novembre

Design team: Carlo Formisano,
Lorenzo De Nicola

General contractor: Tecnobeton

Manufacturers: Almo (furniture),
Bisazza (mosaic), Extralarge
(digital prints), Keope (flooring),
Light Video Sound (lighting)

Total floor area (m²): 300

Opening: October 2001

Photography: Alberto Ferrero

Drop Kick (22-29)

1F, 5-2-14 Roppongi, Minato-ku

Tokyo 105-000

Japan

T +81 3 5786 3420

Open: 9 pm-4 am Mon-Sat

Music: '70s and '80s

Client: Naoki Ito

Interior architect: Glamorous

Design team: Yasumichi Morita,
Akihiro Fujii

General contractor: Mitsui
Designtec

Consultants: Daiko Electric
(lighting), Shoei Ito (graphic
design)

Manufacturers: Lef

Max. capacity: 22

Total floor area (m²): 37

Duration of construction: 5 weeks

Opening: 8 May 2003

Photography: Nacása & Partners

Gravity (70-77)

Jasinskio 16

2600 Vilnius

Lithuania

T +370 5 2497 966

info@clubgravity.lt

www.clubgravity.lt

Open: 10 pm-6 am Fri-Sat

Music: Acid jazz, electro,
drum and bass, house,
progressive house

Dress code: Dress is party-related (orange, white, disco, fetish and so forth)

Client: Andrejara
Designer: Studio Plazma
Design team: Rytis Mikulionis, Evelina Talandzeviciene, Simas Talandzevicius
General contractor: Naresta
Consultants: Donis Indriunas (graphics), Augis Sabaliauskas (lighting)
Manufacturers: Loro
Max. capacity: 400-500
Total floor area (m²): 500
Duration of construction: 6 months
Opening: 6 December 2001
Photography: Raimondas Urbakavichius

Client: Charles Khabouth
Interior architect: munge//leung: design associates
Design team: Sai Leung, Alessandro Munge
General Contractor: Arjeco Industries
Consultants: APEX (A/V), Device (graphics)
Manufacturers: c_ore Architectural Metal, Marcello's Custom Upholstery, Moss & Lam (murals), Platinum Plastics
Max. capacity: 5200
Total floor area (m²): 5274
Total cost (US$): 5,750,000
Budget per m² (US$): 1090
Duration of construction: 2000-2003
Opening: 2000
Photography: David Whittaker

Interior architect: B.inc. interiorstuff
Designer: Eric Kuster
General contractor: Horstermeer interieuren
Consultants: Bartender network (bar supplies), Lightco (ceiling ground floor), P&B Audio (sound system), Henk Schiffmacher (paintings), ...,staat (graphic design, identity and communication)
Manufacturers: Funktion-one, Mark van Holden, Ralph Lauren, Marac, Modular, Sicis, Steelstuff
Max. capacity: 600
Total floor area (m²): 440
Duration of construction: 4 months
Opening: December 2003
Photography: Wouter van den Brink

General contractor: Link Form Interior Design
Engineers: Lee Design Office
Manufacturers: Vitra
Max. capacity: 182 seats
Total floor area (m²): 500
Total cost (¥): 40,000,000
Budget per m² (¥): 80,000
Duration of construction: 5 weeks
Opening: 10 January 2003
Photography: Nacása & Partners

Kabaret's Prophecy (214-221)
16-18 Beak Street
London W1F 9RD
England
T +44 20 7439 2229
info@kabaretsprophecy.com
www.kabaretsprophecy.com
Open: 4 pm-3 am Mon-Fri
Music: Disco, electro-house, hip-hop, house, R&B, reggae

Guvernment (262-269)
132 Queen's Quay East
Toronto M5A 3Y5
Canada
T +1 416 8690 045
info@theguvernment.com
www.theguvernment.com
Open: 10 pm-3 am Thu-Fri; 10 pm-6 am Sat
Music: Breaks beat, groovy house, hip-hop, progressive house, R&B, top-40
Dress code: To impress

Jimmy Woo (142-149)
Korte Leidschedwarsstraat 18
1017 RC Amsterdam
the Netherlands
I +31 20 6263 150
info@jimmywoo.nl
www.jimmywoo.nl
Open: 10 pm-3 am Wed-Thu-Sun; 10 pm-4 am Fri-Sat
Music: Eclectic, hip-hop, urban
Dress code: Chic

Client: Casper Reinders

J-Pop Café Taipei (30-37)
Bistro 98 6-7F, No.98 Sec4
Chong-Xiao E Road
Taipei
Taiwan
T +886 2 2751 2772
www.j-popcafe.com.tw
Open: 11.30 pm-3 am daily
Music: Japanese pop

Client: J-Pop Café
Interior architect: Katsunori Suzuki
Design team: Fantastic Design Works

Interior architect: David Collins
General contractor: PBH
Consultants: Creative Technology (design and integration of the MiPIX LED wall), Jamie Hewlett (bathroom graphics), Chris Levine (lighting), United Visual Artists (LED wall playback, software, programming and operational personnel)
Engineers: PBH
Max. capacity: 150

Total floor area (m²): 225
Duration of construction: 12 weeks
Opening: June 2004
Photography: Adrian Wilson

Kant (182-189)
Kraanplein 6
8000 Brugge
Belgium
T +32 50 3435 31
www.kant-brugge.be
Open: 6 pm-midnight Wed-Sun
Music: Down-tempo lounge to
deep house, with influences of
funk, soul, jazz and gospel

Client: Filip Tijssens
Architect: Ivan Missinne
Design team: Ivan Missinne for
E&L Projects, Ronald Stoops
(photos), Inge Grognard (make up)
General contractor: Eland
Consultants: Artson (sound),
Dark (lighting), Luc Famil
(electricity), Showtex Pandora
(curtains), Ronald Stoops
(art photos), Studioline (photo
prints club walls)
Manufacturers: Domus+ (furniture
and accessories), Debergh
(cutlery), Demomac (kitchen)
Max. capacity: 200
Total floor area (m²): 365
Total cost (€): 350,000
Budget per m² (€): 960

Duration of construction: 4 months
Opening: May 2004
Photography: Studio Verne

Loft (270-277)
Centro San Ignacio, Nivel Vivero
Sector Este, La Castellana
Caracas
Venezuela
T +58 212 267 8998
eventosloft@hotmail.com
Open: 9 pm-6 am Thu-Sat
Music: Disco, electronic, lounge,
merengue, salsa

Client: Grupo AKT 27
Interior architect:
Juan I. Morasso Tucker
Design team: Morasso Arquitectos
General contractor: Grupo AKT 27
Engineer: Henry Hernandez
Max. capacity: 550-600
Facilities: Restaurant
Total floor area (m²): 400
Total investment (US$): 450,000
Budget per m² (US$): 1000
Duration of construction: 7 months
Opening: May 2003
Photography: Andrew Alvarez,
Julio A. Estrada

Lucky Strike Bars (134-141)
La Sip
Rue des Vieux Grenadiers 8-10

1200 Genève
Switzerland
info@lasip.ch
www.lasip.ch
Open: 11.30 pm-4 am Thu;
11.30 pm-5 am Fri-Sat
Music: '80s

Client: British American Tobacco
Switzerland (Lucky Strike)
Interior architect: Atelier Oï
Consultants: Fitch
Manufacturers: Adelta, Ribag
Max. capacity: 600
Duration of construction: 4 months
Opening: Late 2003
Photography: Yves André

Le Cercle
Rue Enning 1
1002 Lausanne
Switzerland
T +41 21 3234 041
info@le-cercle.biz
www.le-cercle.biz
Open: 10 pm-2 am Wed; 10 pm-4
am Thu; 10 pm-5 am Fri-Sat
Music: Electro, house, tech house
(and more)
Client: British American Tobacco
Switzerland (Lucky Strike)
Architect: Konstantin Tzonis
Interior architect: Atelier Oï
Consultants: Fitch
Manufacturers: Adelta, Ribag
Max. capacity: 250-300
Duration of construction: 4 months

Opening: Late 2003
Photography: Yves André

L'Envers
Barre 1
1005 Lausanne
Switzerland
T +41 21 3200 505
message@envers.ch
www.7-bonnes-raisons.ch
Open: 9 pm-2 am Thu-Sat
Music: Various types

Client: British American Tobacco
Switzerland (Lucky Strike)
Interior architect: Atelier Oï
Consultants: Fitch
Manufacturers: Adelta, Ribag
Max. capacity: 200
Duration of construction: 4 months
Opening: Late 2003
Photography: Yves André

Now & Wow (166-173)
Maashaven ZZ 1
3081 AE Rotterdam
the Netherlands
T +31 10 4771 074
info@now-wow.com
www.now-wow.com
Open: 11 pm-6 am Sat
Music: Contemporary tech-house
(Now); eclectic, surprise bands
(Superwow); electro, hip-hop,
rock pop, urban (Wow)

Dress code:
Cool, fool and laid-back

Client: Now & Wow
Interior architect: HUB
Design team: Peter Bosia, Jeroen van Dorsten, Enk van Dijke, Jeroen van der Giessen, Marten de Jong, Remon Lacroix, Ted Langenbach (creative director), Maurice Langstraat, Bob van Lieshout, Pietra Ligura (art direction), Elsbeth van Noppen, Sander den Otter, Rafaël Stolk, Robbert de Vrieze, Martijn van de Wiel
Project management:
Richard van Beusekom,
Koos Hanenberg
General contractor: Hofstede
Consultants: 75B (graphics),
Sander den Otter and Peter Bosia (lighting), Nyo visuals (visual art)
Engineers: IOB
Manufacturers: R3D, JeMaMa (décors), Resign
Max. capacity: 5500
Total floor area (m²): 5000
Total cost (€): 2,100,000
Budget per m² (€): 420
Duration of construction: 6 months
Opening: 14 May 2004
Photography: C.ode Photography,
HUB

Oven (190-197)
Ramón Turró 126
08005 Barcelona
Spain
T +34 932 2108 30
T +34 932 2106 02
eventos@oven.ws
www.oven.ws
Open: 1.30 pm-2 am Mon-Fri;
6 pm-2 am Sat
Music: Acid and chill house,
funk, R&B
Dress code: Smart

Client: Lounge Oven
Architect: Minos Digenis
Arquitectos
Design team: Minos Digenis (principal), Alejandro Bahamon, Enrica Fontana, Patricia Pérez, Alicia Sánchez
Interior designer: Estudi Arola
Design team: Antoni Arola (principal), Sylvain Carlet, Katia Ribas Glossmann, Jordi Tamayo
Graphic design: Pablo Martín
General contractor: Dilor
Consultants: Allpro (sound, lighting), Gràfica (graphics)
Engineers: Dilor (structures, electricity, painting, finishes), SER Acondicionament (air conditioning)
Manufacturers: Alagoas (carpentry), Ca2L, Pavindus (flooring), Santa & Cole, Sillería Verges

Max. capacity: 350 (when used as restaurant: 150 seats)
Total floor area (m²): 600
Total cost (€): 840,000
Budget per m² (€): 1400
Duration of construction: 5 months
Opening: January 2002
Photography: Albert Font, Eugeni Pons

Club Passage (94-101)
Burgring corner
Babenbergerstrasse
1010 Vienna
Austria
T +43 1 9618 800
office@sunshine.at
www.sunshine.at
Open: 8 pm-4 am Wed-Thu;
10 pm-6 am Fri-Sat
Music: House, pop classics (Wed-Fri); premium club music (Sat)
Dress code: Handsome and lovely (Wed-Fri); fancy, funky and trendy (Sat)

Client: Sunshine Enterprises
Interior architects and design team: Söhne & Partner Architekten
General contractor: Söhne & Partner Architekten
Consultants: Bdu (supervision), Christian Ploderer (lighting), Thermo Projekt (MT-services), TIB Altphart (electrical)

Max. capacity: 800
Total floor area (m²): 1500
Total cost (€): 1,000,000
Budget per m² (€): 666
Duration of construction: 12 weeks
Opening: 22 October 2003
Photography: Alexander Koller

Rehab (226-233)
Assembly Street
Leeds LS2 7DE
England
T +44 113 2439 909
info@backtobasics.co.uk
www.backtobasics.co.uk
Open: 10 pm-6 am Sat
Dress code: Smart club wear

Client: Back to Basics
Interior architect: Igloo Design
Design team: John Grant,
Soo Wilkinson
General contractor:
Whitaker & Leach
Consultants: Dave Parry & Fluke
Total floor area (m²): 400
Total cost (£): 350,000
Budget per m² (£): 87.50
Duration of construction: 16 weeks
Opening: September 2002
Photography: Jim Ellam

Sinners (150-157)

Wagenstraat 3

1017 CZ Amsterdam

the Netherlands

T +31 20 6201 375

info@sinners.nl

www.sinners.nl

Open: 11 pm-4 am Thu; 11 pm-
5 am Fri-Sat; 11 pm-4 am Sun

Client: Sinners in Heaven

Interior architect: Ronald Hooft

General contractor: DPD
Doornbosch

Engineers: IJmeer

Manufacturers:
Brandwacht & Meijer

Max. capacity: 300-600

Total floor area (m²): 360

Total cost (€): 1,100,000

Budget per m² (€): 3000

Duration of construction: 4 months

Opening: 1 April 2002

Photography: Jeroen Musch

Sound-Bar (282-289)

226 West Ontario

Chicago, IL 60610

USA

T +1 312 7874 480

sound-bar@sound-bar.com

www.sound-bar.com

Open: 9 pm-4 am Thu-Fri-Sun;
9 pm-5 am Sat

Music: House, pop, techno, trance

Dress code: To impress

Client: MJ Ontario

Interior architect: Slick Design
and Manufacturing

Design team: Amanda Bertucci,
Rocco Laudizio (principal)

General contractor: MAJ
Construction

Consultants: OVT Visuals (visual),
Slick Design and Manufacturing
(lighting), Windmiller Sounds
(audio)

Engineers: Consulting Contraction
Services

Manufacturers: B-K Lighting,
Bitcrafter Media, Bodin
Woodworking, Chicago Floor
Systems, Color Kinetics, Crypton,
Designtex, EDI, Eli, FC Lighting,
G&M Signs, H3 Systems,
Hakatai Enterprises, Halo Lighting,
Independent Neon and Signs,
Interface, Izit Leather, J&A Sheet
Metal, Lithonia Lighting,
Maharam, Piedmont Plastics,
Studio E, Technical Systems,
Tesko, Utrasuede,
Vinta International

Max. capacity: 1200 over two levels

Total floor area (m²): 1850

Total cost (US$): 3,500,000

Budget per m² (US$): 1890

Opening: 1 February 2004

Photography: Michael Dreas

The Spider Club (278-281)

49 West 20th Street

New York, NY 10011

USA

T +1 212 8077 780

Open: 10 pm-4 am Thu-Sun

Music: Alternative

Client: Steve Adelman and
John Blair

Interior architect: d-ash design

Design team: David Ashen,
Christopher Dierig, Ayelet Gezow,
Takushi Yoshida

General contractor: Ideal Interiors

Consultants: Terri Hamilton

Manufacturers: Barrett Hill,
Bisazza, Design Tex, GW
Manufacturing, Kartell, Lane's
Flooring, Maharam, Marrakech,
Nemo Tile, NYC

Max. capacity: 300

Total floor area (m²): 335

Duration of construction: 6 weeks

Opening: November 2003

Photography: Frank Oudeman,
John Horner

Club Stromovka (102-109)

Sport Park Stromovka

Za Císařským mlýnem 33

170 00 Prague 7

Czech Republic

T +420 233 3242 83

recepce@clubrestaurant.cz

www.clubrestaurant.cz

Open: 10 am-11 pm Mon-Sun

Music: Brazilian electro, c-lounge,
chill out, Latin

Client: Tennis Stromovka

Interior architect: Atelier Kunc

Design team: Halina Keilová,
Michal Kunc (principal),
Daniel Pospíšil, Lukáš Zimandl,
Vendula Zimandlová

General contractor: LOCI interier

Max. capacity: 180

Total floor area (m²): 240

Duration of construction: 4 months

Opening: January 2004

Photography: Tomáš Rasl

Supperclub Amsterdam (158-165)

Jonge Roelensteeg 21

1012 PL Amsterdam

the Netherlands

T +31 20 3446 404

info@supperclub.nl

www.supperclub.nl

Open: 7 pm-1 am Sun-Thu;
9 pm-3 am Fri-Sat

Music: Lounge

Dress code: Chic, cool, funky,
sexy, trendy

Client: IQ Creative

Interior architect: Concrete
Architectural Associates

Project team: Rob Wagemans,
Gilian Schrofer, Erik van Dillen

Manufacturers: Atlas, Bont,
Fairlight, Mammoet Horeca,
Provid, Smederij van Rijn,
Ubachs Betimmeringen, Vasco,
Vitra Point
Consultants: Atmosphere Lighting
(light), Joppe Claassen Video
(video and sound)
Max. capacity: 300
Total area (m²): 400
Opening: October 1999

Supperclub Cruise
Travelling different locations
the Netherlands
T +31 20 3446 404
info@supperclub.nl
www.supperclubcruise.nl

Client: IQ Creative and
Healers & Beads
Interior architect: Concrete
Architectural Associates
Project team: Rob Wagemans,
Gilian Schrofer, Erik van Dillen,
Joris Angevaare
Manufacturers: Bont, Faries,
H2B houtbewerking en Interieur,
Jozef & Zn., Schouten, Ubachs
Betimmeringen, Vasco, Vermeulen
Kunststoftoepassingen,
Wijnheymer
Consultants: Ampco-Flashlight
(light and sound), F.A. Consultant
(shipbuilding)
Max. capacity: 255
Total area (m²): 350

Duration of construction: 14 weeks
Opening: 10 October 2003

Supperclub Rome
Via de' Nari 14
00186 Roma
Italy
T +39 06 6880 7207
reservation@supperclub.com
www.supperclub.com
Open: 8.30 pm-late Mon-Sun;
closed in August

Client: IQ Creative
Interior architect: Concrete
Architectural Associates
Project team: Rob Wagemans,
Gilian Schrofer, Erik van Dillen
Manufacturers: Loggere, Smederij
van Rijn, Ubachs Betimmeringen
Consultants: Ampco-Flashlight
(light and sound)
Max. capacity: 500
Total area (m²): 418
Opening: 6 October 2002

Club Tallinn (78-85)
Narva mnt 27
51013 Tartu
Estonia
T +372 7 4031 57
clubtallinn@clubtallinn.ee
www.clubtallinn.ee
Open: 10 pm-4 am Thu-Sat

Music: Break beat, drum and bass,
hip-hop, house
Dress code: Casual club clothes

Client: Meelispaik
Interior architect: Kohvi
Design team: Hannes Praks,
Villem Valme
Consultants: Kohvi (lighting),
Nafta Llc (A/V), Vanzetti (graphics)
Engineers: Toomas Valdmann
Furniture: Tartu Puukoda, Univa
Max. capacity: 1200
Total floor area (m²): 990
Total cost (€): 190,000
Budget per m² (€): 190
Duration of construction: 4 months
Opening: September 2003
Photography: Vahur Puik

Thin (290-297)
852 Fifth Avenue
San Diego, CA 92101
USA
T +1 619 2355 616
greg@lwpgroup.com
www.thinroom.com
Open: 7 pm-2 am Tue-Sat
Music: Deep house, electronic,
hip-hop, progressive house,
trip hop, rare grooves
Dress code: Smart

Client: LWP Group
Interior architect: Graham Downes

Architecture
Design team: Graham Downes
(principal), Jeanette Boettcher,
Eva Thorn
General contractor: Mike Pandolfe
Consultants: Pool (graphic and
environmental design)
Engineers: D. Lowen Electric,
Ideal Mechanic, James Houghton
Plumbing
Manufacturers: Abbas, Basille
Studio
Max. capacity: 240
Total floor area (m²): 3616
Total cost (US$): 1,300,000
Duration of construction: 6 months
Opening: January 2003
Photography: Tim Mantoani

Touch (46-53)
1st Floor, Trendset Towers
Road No. 2, Banjara Hills
Hyderabad 500034
India
T +91 40 2354 2433
T +91 40 5551 6666
Open: 9 pm-midnight Mon-Thu;
7 pm-3 am Fri-Sat
Music: Fusion, lounge, progressive
house, upbeat lounge

Client: Nagarjuna and
Preetam Reddy
Architects: Khosla Associates
Design team: Amaresh Anand,

Anshul Chodha, Madhavi C,
Sandeep Khosla (principal)
General contractor: Scales Intech
Interiors
Consultants: Kaize Patel (kitchen
and bar), Raghunath & sons
(electrical), Reiz Electrocontrols
(lighting), Sriram Comforts
Systems (HVAC), Tania Khosla
Design (graphics)
Manufacturers: Ikian (Furniture),
Metro Enterprises (aluminium and
steel), Neospar Concept (resin
accessories), Smith Interiors
Max. capacity: 300-350
Total floor area (m^2): 427
Total cost (US$): 454,000
Budget per m^2 (US$): 1063
Duration of construction: 6 months
Opening: February 2004
Photography: Pallon Daruwala

Architects

3deluxe (118-125)
Schwalbacher Strasse 74
65183 Wiesbaden
Germany
T +49 611 9522 05-0
F +49 611 9522 05-22
info@3deluxe.de
www.3deluxe.de

Atelier Kunc (102-109)
Komunardu 43
170 00 Holešovice Prague 7
Czech Republic
T +420 602 3674 48
F +420 220 8073 04
atelierkunc@atelierkunc.com
www.atelierkunc.com

**Atelier Oï Architecture and Design
(134-141)**
Signolet 3
2520 La Neuveville
Switzerland
T +41 32 7515 666
contact@atelier-oi.ch
www.atelier-oi.ch

B.inc. interiorstuff (142-149)
Naarderstraat 17
1251 AX Laren
the Netherlands
T +31 35 5318 773
info@binc.nl
www.binc.nl

David Collins (214-221)
79 Farm Lane
London SW6 1QA
England
T +44 20 7835 5000
www.davidcollins.com

**Concrete Architectural Associates
(158-165)**
Rozengracht 133-3
1016 LV Amsterdam
the Netherlands
T +31 20 5200 200
F +31 20 5200 201
info@concrete.archined.nl
www.concrete.archined.nl

d-ash design (278-281)
43-40 34th Street, 2nd Floor
Long Island City, NY 11101
USA
T +1 718 3832 225
dashen@davidashendesign.com
www.davidashendesign.com

**Ivan Missinne for E&L Projects
(182-189)**
Kennedypark 16b
8500 Kortrijk
Belgium
T +32 56 2030 76
F +32 56 2046 78
ivan.missinne@E-L.be
www.E-L.be

Estudi Arola (190-197)
Lope de Vega, 106, 3°
08005 Barcelona
Spain
T +34 93 3075 369
info@estudiarola.com
www.estudiarola.com

**Fantastic Design Works
(30-37)**
401-5-18-4 Maison-Minami-
Aoyama, Minami-Aoyama, Minato-ku
Tokyo 107-0062
Japan
T +81 3 5778 0178
tokyo@f-fantastic.com
www.f-fantastic.com

Geomim Design (62-69)
Tesvikiye Cad. 95, D:5 Tesvikiye
80200 Istanbul
Turkey
T +90 212 2365 704
geomim@geomim.com
www.geomim.com

Glamorous (22-29)
1F, 7-6 Omasu-cho, Ashiya
Hyogo 659-0066
Japan
T +81 797 2367 70
info@glamorous.co.jp
www.glamorous.co.jp

Glenn Sestig Architects (174-181)
Fortlaan 1
9000 Ghent
Belgium

T +32 9 2401 190
contact@glennsestigarchitects.com
www.glennsestigarchitects.com

**Graham Downes Architecture
(290-297)**
1600 National Avenue
San Diego, CA 92113
USA
T +1 619 2342 565
F +1 619 2342 568
gda@blokhaus.com
www.blokhaus.com

Graven Images (242-245)
83a Candleriggs
Glasgow G1 1LF
Scotland
T +44 141 5526 626
F +44 141 5520 433
info@graven.co.uk
www.graven.co.uk

Hazard Studio (222-225)
11 Urb El Montico
24196 Leon
Spain
T + 34 6 4988 7397
4, rue de Louvois
75002 Paris
T +33 1 4296 3868
alfredo@hazardstudio.com
www.hazardstudio.com

**Holzer Kobler Architekturen
(126-133)**
Ankerstrasse 3

Switzerland

T +41 1 2405 200

mail@holzerkobler.ch

www.holzerkobler.ch

Ronald Hooft (150-157)

Nieuwendammerkade 28 a2

1022 AB Amsterdam

the Netherlands

T +31 20 6381 197

F +31 20 5285 139

rhooft@xs4all.nl

HUB (166-173)

the Netherlands

T +31 10 4846 180

info@hubcreative.nl

www.hubcreative.nl

**ICRAVE Design Studio
(254-261)**

220 West 19th Street, 11th floor

New York, NY 10011

USA

T +1 212 9295 657

info@icravedesign.com

www.icravedesign.com

Igloo Design (226-233)

44 Ledburn Court

Manchester M15 4HR

England

T +44 161 8326 793

soo@igloodesign.co.uk

www.igloodesign.co.uk

Khosla Associates (46-53)

18, 17th Main, HAL II A Stage,

Indiranagar

560 008 Bangalore

India

T +91 80 2529 4951

info@khoslaassociates.com

www.khoslaassociates.com

Kohvi (78-85)

Narva mnt 68-1

10127 Tallinn

Estonia

T +372 5 2736 26

kohvi@kohvirecords.ee

www.kohvi.com

Lief Design (234-241)

17 Broad Street

Nottingham NG1 3AJ

England

T +44 115 9529 020

info@lief.co.uk

www.lief.co.uk

**Minos Digenis Arquitectos
(190-197)**

Pallars 160 bis

08005 Barcelona

Spain

T +34 93 3208 050

F +34 93 3208 052

Morasso Arquitectos (270-277)

Av. Circunvalacion del Sol, Centro

Profesional Santa Paula

Torre A, Piso 1, Ofic. 13

Caracas

Venezuela

T +58 212 9869 589

M +58 416 6066 738

juanmorasso@cantv.net

info@morasso-arquitectos.com

www.morasso-arquitectos.com

**Mueller Kneer Associates
(206-213)**

18-20 Scrutton Street

London EC2A 4EN

England

T +44 20 7247 0993

F +44 20 7247 9935

info@muellerkneer.com

www.muellerkneer.com

**munge//leung: design associates
(262-269)**

249 Dufferin Street

Toronto M6K 1Z5

Canada

T +1 416 5881 668

info@mungeleung.com

www.mungeleung.com

Fabio Novembre (110-117)

Via Mecenate 76/3

20138 Milan

Italy

T +39 02 5041 04

F +39 02 5023 75

info@novembre.it

www.novembre.it

Ora-ïto (198-205)

320, rue St-Honoré

75001 Paris

France

T +33 1 4246 0009

info@ora-ito.com

www.ora-ito.com

Orbit Design Studio (38-45)

Unit 2a, M. Thai Tower, All

Seasons Place, 87 Wireless Road

10330 Bangkok

Thailand

T +66 2 6543 667

christopher@orbitdesignstudio.com

www.orbitdesignstudio.com

Studio Plazma (70-77)

Gedimino pr. 28/2-808

2000 Vilnius

Lithuania

T +370 5 2610 885

info@plazma.lt

www.plazma.lt

Muti Randolph (246-253)

Praia de Botafogo, 68/601

RJ 22250-040, Rio de Janeiro

Brazil

T +55 21 2551 2692

mi@muti.cx

www.muti.cx

**Savinkin/Kuzmin project group
(54-61)**

Spiridonovka 30/1

103001 Moscow

Russia
T +70 9 5956 8267
poledesign@umail.ru

SJB Interiors (14-21)
25 Coventry Street, Southbank
Melbourne
Victoria 3006
Australia
T +61 3 9686 2122
interiors@sjb.com.au
www.sjb.com.au

**Slick Design and Manufactering
(282-289)**
941 West Randolph Street
Chicago, IL 60607
USA
T +1 312 5639 000
F +1 312 5639 008
inquiries@slickdesign.com
www.slickdesign.com

**Söhne & Partner Architekten
(94-101)**
Mariahilferstrasse 101, Hof 3,
Stiege 4, Top 47
1060 Vienna
Austria
T +43 1 9524 402
office@soehne-partner.com
www.soehne-partner.com

Photographers

Andrew Alvarez (270-277)
andrewphoto@cantv.net

Yves André (134-141)
T +41 32 8355 060

Marq Bailey (206-213)
T +44 7958 2021 32
contact@marqb.net

Wouter van den Brink (142-149)
T +31 6 2181 5419
woutervandenbrink@par31.com
www.par31.com

Francisco Carrascosa (126-133)
T +41 1 4404 095
F +41 1 2787 880
M +41 79 6838 551
paco.c@bluewin.ch

Stéphane Chalmeau (222-225)
M +33 6 1080 5914
F +33 2 4047 5069
chalmeau.igloo@wanadoo.fr

C.oDe Photography (169)
T +31 15 2624 964
code.coen@planet.nl

Rolant Dafis (206-213)
T +44 20 8531 5003
T +44 77 1163 5206
rolant.morgan@virgin.net

Pallon Daruwala (46-53)

Yavuz Draman (62-69)
T +90 212 2634 477
www.yavuzdraman.com

Michael Dreas (282-289)
info@michaeldreas.com
www.michaeldreas.com

Jim Ellam (226-233)
T +44 79 7393 3801

Julio A. Estrada (270-277)
estradajulio@yahoo.com

Alberto Ferrero (110-117)
M +39 348 3153 153
F +39 02 5681 8638
mail@albertoferrero.it
www.albertoferrero.it

Rômulo Fialdini (246-253)

Albert Font (195)
T +34 932 3786 10
foto@albertfont.com
www.albertfont.com

Jean-Pierre Gabriel (174-181)
T +32 2 6404 818
F +32 2 6463 693
jp@jpgl.be

Marcus Görtz (38-45)

John Horner (278-281)

T +1 617 4844 786

horner.john@verizon.net

Laurence Hudghton (234-241)

T +44 161 2727 977

laurence@hudghtonphotography.co.uk

Keith Hunter (242-245)

T +44 141 8864 503

F +44 141 8864 509

Alexander Koller (94-101)

T/F +43 1 9575 824

M +43 699 1046 2824

office@alexanderkoller.com

www.alexanderkoller.com

Tim Mantoani (290-297)

T +1 619 5439 959

Tony Miller (14-21)

T +61 412 5355 75

archphoto@ihug.com.au

Jeroen Musch (150-157)

T/F +31 20 6184 152

mail@jeroenmusch.nl

www.jeroenmusch.nl

Nacása & Partners

(22-29, 30-37)

T +81 3 5722 7757

F +81 3 5722 0909

partners@nacasa.co.jp

www.nacasa.co.jp

Frank Oudeman

(254-261, 278-281)

T +1 212 6745 826

frankoudeman@earthlink.net

K. Ovchinnikov (54-61)

T +7 9 1611 30374

kirill-krokodill@list.ru

Eugeni Pons (190-197)

T/F +34 97 2372 505

info@eugeni-pons.com

www.eugeni-pons.com

Vahur Puik (78-85)

puik@bumpclub.ee

Emanuel Raab (114-121)

T +49 611 8427 06

F +49 611 8019 52

Tomáš Rasl (98-105)

T +420 603 9710 45

tomasrasl@seznam.cz

Raimondas Urbakavichius (70-77)

T +370 68 7260 39

raimondas.u@mail.lt

Studio Verne (182-189)

T +32 9 2334 855

F +32 9 2334 093

info@verne.be

www.verne.be

David Whittaker (262-269)

T +1 416 4290 245

F +1 416 9307 789

Adrian Wilson (214-221)

T +1 212 7297 077

M +44 7831 2017 46

adrian.wilson@virgin.net

www.interiorphotography.net

Colophon

Night Fever:
Interior Design for Bars and Clubs

Publishers
Frame Publishers
www.framemag.com
Birkhäuser – Publishers
for Architecture
www.birkhauser.ch

Compiled by the editors of
Frame magazine

Written by Matthew Stewart

Sponsor
ABSOLUT

Graphic design
…,staat
www.staatamsterdam.nl

Copy editing
Donna de Vries-Hermansader

Colour reproduction
Reproscan, the Netherlands

Printing
Star Standard, Singapore

Distribution
Benelux, China, Japan,
Korea and Taiwan
ISBN 90-77174-04-4
Frame Publishers
Lijnbaansgracht 87
1015 GZ Amsterdam
the Netherlands
info@framemag.com
www.framemag.com

All other countries
ISBN 3-7643-0512-6
Birkhäuser – Publishers
for Architecture
PO Box 133
4010 Basel
Switzerland
Part of Springer
Science+Business Media
www.birkhauser.ch

© 2005 Frame Publishers
© 2005 Birkhäuser – Publishers
for Architecture

A CIP catalogue record for this
book is available from the Library of
Congress, Washington, D.C., USA

Bibliographic information
published by
Die Deutsche Bibliothek
Die Deutsche Bibliothek lists this
publication in the Deutsche
Nationalbibliografie; detailed
bibliographic data is available on
the internet at http://dnb.ddb.de.

Printed on acid-free paper
produced from chlorine-free pulp.
TCF ∞
Printed in Singapore
987654321